The FINDHORN FAMILY COOK BOOK

The FINDHORN FAMILY COOK BOOK

*a vegetarian cookbook which celebrates
the wholeness of life*

KAY LYNNE SHERMAN

SHAMBHALA
BOULDER 1982

SHAMBHALA PUBLICATIONS, INC.
1920 13th Street
Boulder, Colorado 80302

Distributed in the United States by Random House
and in Canada by Random House of Canada, Ltd.

Printed in the United States of America.

Library of Congress Cataloging in Publication Data

Main entry under title:

The Findhorn family cookbook.

 Originally published: Findhorn, Scotland : Findhorn
Publications, 1981.
 Includes index.
 1. Vegetarian cookery, I. Sherman, Kay Lynne.
TX837.F47 1982   641.5'636   81-84324
ISBN 0-87773-219-1 (pbk.)
ISBN 0-394-70888-1 (Random House : pbk.)

For Eileen and Joannie, the original Findhorn cooks.
They inspire us all.

Design: Neil Baird, Hilary Baird, Linda Morris
Cover Design: Linda Morris
Illustrations and Calligraphy: Linda Morris
Photography: Kathy Thormod

Grateful thanks to the many people who have contributed
to the creation of this cookbook. All, in addition to doing
their jobs superbly, have also contributed in support and
friendship. Sandra Kramer has painstakingly edited and proof-
read the copy; Sharon Quiring has done all of the original
typing (somehow deciphering the worst scribbles). Help in
printing photographs has been given by Helen-Ruth Fisher;
typesetting done by the old 'pro' Charles Petersen, and by
Peter Königs; darkroom work by Chryss Craswell, Gareth
Rostoker and Arthur Bailey. Thanks to Phil Innes for printing
the cover; to Elizabeth Schnadt, Charles Adkinson and Bruce
Bulloch for their essential help with artwork; and to Tim
Moore for his humour and moral support in the Design Studio.
A special thanks to Suzette Curtis for her advice on the design,
to John ('How is the writing going?') Button for keeping us
on schedule in a friendly but determined manner, to Edwin
Maynard for the use of the photograph on page 105, to David
McNamara for the use of the photographs on pages 93, 95,
101 top, and to Will Elwell for the use of the photograph on
page 9.

Thanks to the creative cooks of Findhorn who have
contributed recipes: Loren Stewart. Vadan Baker, Ike and
Maggie Isaksen, Mary Coulman, Jacques Cormier, Richard
Valeriano, Erik Muller, Bill Flink, Peter Caddy, Ludja Bolla,
Pam O'Neill, Bob Knox, Frances Edwards, Maggie Miller,
Deborah Horner, Jeff Dienst, Shelley Drogin, Lynn Imperatore,
Rennie Innis, Bessie Schadee, Debi DeMarco, Clara Bianca
Erede, and Sabrina Dearborn.

And my personal thanks to David and Alexandra and
Ludja for keeping me laughing; to Erik for his steadfast
support; to John Freed: head gopher and dear friend; to
Linda Morris and Kathy Thormod, who helped me to conceive
the original idea, and whose friendship and professional skill
I value deeply; and finally to the Findhorn Community itself,
which has nurtured and supported the creation of this book.

Table of Contents

Necessary Information for Using this Book

Measuring:

The recipes are presented in metric, Imperial and American measurements. In the case of Imperial measurement, it has been more exact to use fluid ounce measures than pints in many cases, so it will be necessary to have a measuring jug which measures fluid ounces. As all measurements are standard, please use measuring spoons, cups and scales rather than guessing. All tablespoon and teaspoon measurements are meant to be level measures. AMERICAN TEASPOONS, TABLESPOONS, CUPS AND PINTS ARE A DIFFERENT SIZE TO BRITISH ONES, so if you look across the page and notice a different amount, that is the reason.

Ingredients:

Herbs—all herbs are dried, rather than fresh, unless specified otherwise.

Milk Powder—non-instant milk powder has been used in these recipes.

Miso—fermented soya bean paste used as soup broth base and as seasoning. Available in many different flavours from whole food shops. Any one of the flavours will do in these recipes.

Tamari—a natural soya sauce of very good quality, usually available in whole food shops.

Tofu—soya bean curd. For more information refer to the *Tofu* section.

*It is good to prepare vegetables with real appreciation
for what you are doing, thus enabling the radiations of light
to enter the food. A potato is no longer just a potato
in your hands, but a thing of real beauty. You can feel it is
something living, vibrating. Just stop and think what a difference
this makes to the vegetables. Sometimes you feel
your heart will burst with joy and appreciation.*

Eileen's guidance

Visitors to our community often find themselves enjoying vegetarian cooking for the first time during their stay. As a result, we have been asked again and again to publish a cookbook; the book in your hands is the response to that request.

Although we regularly cook for very large numbers of people, we felt it would be more useful to the average person to present family-sized recipes.

Once the decision was made to publish a cookbook, then began the joyful task of collecting and writing recipes. The inspired cooks of the community have opened their notebooks, kitchens and hearts to the creation of this cookbook. For example, everyone said, "Mary Coulman makes the best sherry trifles; she also makes the best bikkies." So I asked Mary if I could have some of her recipes, knowing that very often good cooks are reluctant to give up their secrets. She graciously invited me over for tea that lasted till suppertime, loaned me her hand-written notebook of favourite recipes, then spent considerable time adding the minute details. While I was testing recipes, she came by to make very sure that I had done them correctly. And that experience has been repeated over and over again with many cooks and many kitchens. Here we are presenting to you some simple everyday fare, as well as special occasion favourites, the product of creativity and joy-filled celebrations.

The other aspect of writing the cookbook has been to find ways to communicate the more subtle ideas behind the way we prepare food; the idea of enjoying whatever work we do, of bringing Spirit into matter.

Linda's artwork and Kathy's photography have brought those ideas to life in a way that far surpasses mere words. And the extracts from guidance received by either Eileen Caddy or David Spangler, which introduce most of the chapters, have served to inspire us. What we wish to share is that the most important ingredient that goes into any meal is the love with which it is prepared. Love has the ability of lifting and transforming every meal and every situation.

Kay Lynne

Cooks and Their Environment

One thing we notice at Findhorn is that the attitude of the cooks has a tremendous effect on the whole community. It is a pivotal job, and must not be performed by someone who considers it to be a drudgery. The same is certainly true in every home. The consciousness you bring to the job is transferred to the food, and from there to your family. So cooking is really a way of giving; a daily ritual of bringing Spirit into matter.

The physical environment is important, and creating a kitchen that is light and loving is a joyful task. Start by meditation or spending some quiet, undisturbed time there. And occasionally notice what parts of the kitchen need some attention. If an entirely new environment needs to be created, clean and paint the whole place. Get rid of stale food. Organise things. Put the herbs and spices in alphabetical order. There needs to be order to things, an order like that in nature: appearing to be spontaneous on the surface, but working very smoothly and in perfect rhythm underneath.

Each tool you work with becomes a good friend if you take care of it and learn how to use it appropriately. Quality is preferred to quantity in kitchen equipment: better to have one very good knife than a whole set of mediocre ones.

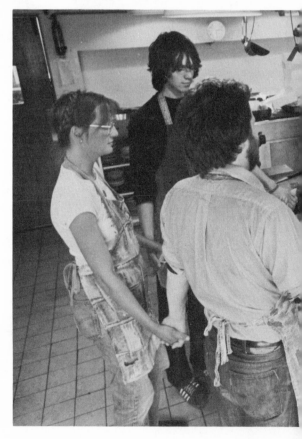

When equipping a kitchen, keep in mind the people who will be using it. If children like to help, it's nice to have some tools that are safe enough for them. If the kitchen is used by a large number of people, it's preferable to have simple, indestructible equipment rather than sophisticated gadgets.

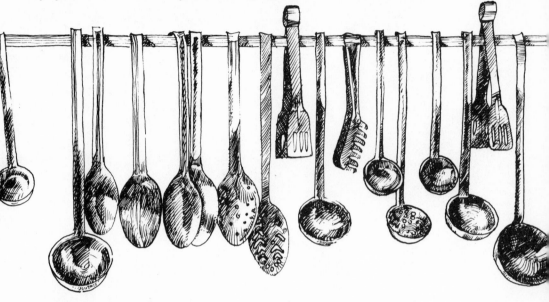

Wooden beings (spoons, cutting boards) should be protected from soapy water and strong flavours, as they absorb everything. Wash them immediately after using; dry, and put away. Don't leave the spoon to cook in the soup; it doesn't do the soup or the spoon any good. The wooden handles on knives deteriorate if they are left to soak, and the knife blade is dulled when it hits against other things in soapy water. So wash the knife immediately after use and put away. Wooden boards should be lightly oiled if they become dry.

Metal beings (frying pans, wok, saucepans) should not be left to soak in water if they are made of iron, as it too absorbs flavours and tends to rust. If iron pans are treated well, they will need only a quick wiping out after use. If they do need cleaning, follow the method described for the omelette pan, in the omelette recipe. If pans become dried out, season them with oil. Slowly heat oil in the pan for 20 minutes, then pour it out and wipe the pan clean. Woks should be washed with water only and a stiff brush, immediately after use. This energy invested in your kitchen and in the tools you use will reap the rewards of efficiency and pleasure in cooking.

Soups

*We are seeking to nourish your consciousness
to move into Oneness. This does not mean that you ignore
the wisdom of a proper diet, but that you include
the most important ingredients which are awareness and love.*

David Spangler, 12 August 1971,
transmission on kitchen & food

It's an interesting phenomenon that people often make the best soups when they're out of all the things they normally cook with. Soups are an expression of creativity; recipes are the starting point, the inspiration.

Loren, one of our best soup cooks, moved to Erraid, an island we caretake, off the west coast of Scotland. There is much less variety of food available there than here, yet visitors declare that he's become an even greater soup cook since he moved. Making soups often goes with getting back to basics, and whether simple cooking is by choice or by force of circumstance, the result is often better cooking.

Ludja, our resident Czechoslovakian sage, quotes her mother: "To cook when you have all the ingredients, that is nothing. When you don't have the ingredients, that is something."

Stocks

Using vegetable stock as a base for soups really does make a difference! Here are some relatively effortless ways to make vegetable stock.

Method No. 1
Save the bits and pieces that are usually discarded from vegetables. Often the peelings and the most flavourful parts of carrots, greens, celery, cabbage, cauliflower, etc. get thrown away. Mushroom bits, onion skins and potato peelings are particularly valuable for their colour and flavour. As you are preparing a meal save those bits. Put them in a saucepan, cover them with cold water and let simmer gently on the back of the stove for at least 20 minutes. Turn off the heat, and let sit until cool. Pour through a strainer into a jar and keep in the refrigerator until you need it, or use immediately.

Method No. 2
Save your vegetable cooking water. Keep it in a jar in the refrigerator until soup-making time. Caution: Don't add hot stock to the cold, as this seems to spoil it; rather, let the stock cool down first. Cooking water from any vegetable may be used, with the exception of beetroot, which gives a strong colour to the broth.

Method No. 3
For those times when you are caught without stock, have a commercial substitute on hand. Miso or tamari can be added to soup to give it flavour, as can yeast extract, Marmite (British) or powdered vegetable broth. These, however, are emergency items only!

Making a Better Soup

The most important rule is TASTE THE SOUP. If you find it lacking, here are some suggestions:

To give it body, flavour and zip, add one or more of the following:

salt

miso

vegetable stock powder

tamari

Marmite

yeast extract

sautéed onions

sautéed celery leaves

Spices
coriander, cumin, cloves

Herbs
basil, marjoram, lovage, thyme, bay, parsley, celery, oregano

butter

milk or cream

lemon juice

garlic

left-over sauce or gravy

To thicken it, follow one of these methods:
1. Mix a bit of flour, arrowroot or cornflour (cornstarch) with cold water, and add to the soup.
2. Make a roux of butter and flour; after cooking for 5 minutes, whisk into soup. ·
3. Blend a portion of the soup.
4. Blend left-over spaghetti with water and add to soup.

To make the soup look appealing, use one or more of the following as a topping:

parsley

grated cheese

spring onions, chopped

croûtons

chives, finely chopped

slivered avocado

chopped cucumber

any colourful vegetable, slivered very thin

paprika

nutmeg

gomasio

roasted nuts or seeds

The Simplest Soup

METRIC/IMPERIAL

a fresh vegetable in
season

a slice of onion and
a few celery leaves

good vegetable stock

butter

salt

milk

1. Wash and chop vegetables.
2. In a saucepan cover vegetables with stock. Bring to a boil, then simmer until tender.
3. Spoon vegetables, stock and a lump of butter into blender. Process until completely smooth.
4. Return to saucepan and heat to just under boiling point. Add water if needed and check to see if salt needs to be added.
5. Before serving add a bit of milk—just enough to make the soup turn a lighter colour. Do not allow to boil after adding milk!

AMERICAN

a fresh vegetable in
season

a slice of onion and
a few celery leaves

good vegetable stock

butter

salt

milk

Suggestion
This is a good way to use little bits of leftover vegetables.
Just heat them with their cooking water, then follow steps 3-5.

Cream of Tomato Soup

METRIC/IMPERIAL

570ml/1 pint milk

450g/1 lb very red,
ripe tomatoes

30g/1oz butter

2 Tbsp flour

1 tsp salt

1 tsp honey

1 thin slice onion

1 sliver of garlic

Makes 4 servings

A refreshing first course

1. Hold tomatoes with a fork over heat until skin blisters. Immerse in cold water. Peel.
2. Heat milk in a saucepan.
3. In a blender, blend all ingredients except milk, until smooth.
4. With blender running, slowly and carefully pour in hot milk.
5. Return mixture to saucepan and heat to serving temperature. DO NOT ALLOW TO BOIL!
6. Serve immediately.

AMERICAN

2 cups milk

2½ cups very red,
ripe tomatoes

2 Tbsp butter

2 Tbsp flour

1 tsp salt

1 tsp honey

1 thin slice onion

1 sliver of garlic

Makes 4 servings

Suggestion
Most of the preparation for this soup can be done in advance:
have all ingredients ready in the blender and milk in a saucepan.
The soup tastes its best when blended and heated immediately before serving.

Cream of Cauliflower

METRIC/IMPERIAL

30g/1oz chopped onions

60g/2oz chopped celery and leaves

2 Tbsp butter or oil

450g/1 lb cauliflower, washed and cut into pieces

water to cover

60g/2oz butter

4 Tbsp flour

½ litre/1 pint cooking water

salt

4 Tbsp milk or cream

4 egg yolks (optional)

parsley, nutmeg, paprika or hard-cooked egg for topping

Makes 4 servings

AMERICAN

¼ cup chopped onions

½ cup chopped celery and leaves

2 Tbsp butter or oil

1 medium cauliflower, washed and cut into pieces

water to cover

¼ cup butter

¼ cup flour

2 cups cooking water

salt

¼ cup milk or cream

4 egg yolks (optional)

parsley, nutmeg, paprika or hard-cooked egg for topping

Makes 4 servings

1. In a saucepan, heat the oil. Fry onions and celery until translucent.
2. Add water and cauliflower. Bring to a boil, then simmer until tender.
3. Drain water from cauliflower, saving the cooking liquid. Put a few flowerettes aside. Into a blender put cauliflower, onions, celery and enough water to purée easily. Blend until smooth.
4. In a saucepan, melt butter and whisk in the flour. Cook slowly for 5 minutes, stirring occasionally.
5. Add ½ litre/1 pint/2 cups cooking water. Simmer until thickened, stirring with a whisk.
6. Add puréed vegetables to sauce, taste soup, and add salt if needed.
7. Just before serving, add milk or cream and bring to serving temperature, being careful not to boil the soup.
8. (Optional) For added richness, stir a small amount of soup into beaten egg yolks; return to soup.
9. Put a few flowerettes in each soup bowl, then the soup. Top with nutmeg, paprika or chopped parsley.

Emergency

If you really are short on time, omit the step of making the sauce separately. After cooking the vegetables, put them with their cooking water plus butter and flour into the blender and purée everything. Return to saucepan and add water if needed; then cook for 5 minutes. Add milk and eggs, and serve.

Variations

This recipe can be used with many different vegetables; some good ones are asparagus, leeks, spinach, carrots, courgettes (zucchini), mushrooms or cabbage. Use what you have.
For a non-dairy soup, omit milk and eggs.

Grandmother's Vegetable Barley Soup

METRIC/IMPERIAL

1 onion

inner stalks of a head of celery

2 Tbsp oil

2¼ litres/4 pints water

170g/6oz barley

1 bay leaf

2 medium potatoes

2 carrots

860g/1 lb 14oz tin tomatoes

225g/8oz green vegetable in season (e.g. courgettes or green beans)

1 tsp basil

1 Tbsp salt

Makes 10-12 servings

1. Chop onion, celery and leaves; then fry them in oil, in a large soup pot.
2. When vegetables are tender and beginning to brown, add water. Bring to a boil.
3. Rinse barley under running water, then add to boiling soup stock. Add bay leaf and simmer until barley is tender, about one hour.
4. Chop potatoes, carrots and tomatoes.
5. Add potatoes, carrots, tomatoes and tomato juice to soup; simmer until vegetables are completely done and beginning to get mushy, about an hour. If water boils away, add more.
6. Add green vegetables and basil at the last. Cook until vegetables are just tender.
7. Taste, and add salt if necessary.

Serving Suggestion

This is a hearty soup, which needs only a salad and homemade bread to complete the meal. Serve topped with chopped parsley or grated cheese.

AMERICAN

1 onion

inner stalks of a head of celery

2 Tbsp oil

2½ quarts water

1 cup barley

1 bay leaf

2 medium potatoes

2 carrots

1 lb 14oz can tomatoes

1½ cups chopped green vegetable in season (e.g. zucchini or green beans)

1 tsp basil

1 Tbsp salt

Makes 10-12 servings

Variation: Italian Minestrone

1. Use olive oil to fry onions and celery.
2. In place of barley, cook the equal amount of kidney beans and 1 tsp. sage.
3. At the end, with the green vegetables and basil, add 110g/4oz noodles and 1 tsp oregano. Cook until noodles are tender.
4. Use parmesan or romano cheese, and grate it fresh. Top each serving with grated cheese.

Hearty Bean Soup

This is the basic recipe for lentils, dried beans or split peas. Make it in large quantity, as it improves with age and can be used as a base for other soups.

METRIC/IMPERIAL

1 onion

4 cloves garlic

4 stalks celery and leaves

2 Tbsp oil

2¼ litres/4 pints water

1 tsp sage

1 bay leaf

450g/1 lb dried beans

Binding

4 Tbsp butter or oil

4 Tbsp flour

½ litre/1 pint water

3 tsp salt

Makes 6-8 servings

AMERICAN

1 onion

4 cloves garlic

4 stalks celery and leaves

2 Tbsp oil

2½ quarts water

1 tsp sage

1 bay leaf

2½ cups dried beans

Binding

4 Tbsp butter or oil

¼ cup flour

2 cups water

3 tsp salt

Makes 6-8 servings

1. Peel and chop onion and garlic. Wash and chop celery, leaves and all.
2. In a large soup pot, heat oil; then sauté onion, garlic and celery until golden.
3. Add stock or water, bay leaf and sage; bring to a boil. Wash and sort beans, then add to water and bring to a boil again. Turn off heat and wait until beans sink to the bottom (about 15 minutes). If you have soaked beans overnight, this step may be omitted.
4. Simmer beans gently until tender. The time varies from 2 to 4 hours, depending on the type of bean. If you have a slow cooker (crock pot), a wood stove or an Aga with a very slow heat, let the soup cook overnight, or all day. It seems the longer this soup cooks, the better it tastes.
5. When beans are well cooked and beginning to get mushy, prepare the binding. Heat butter or oil in a small saucepan, add flour and cook slowly for 5 minutes, stirring occasionally. Then add water and salt and bring to a boil, stirring constantly. Pour into soup. If the soup has been cooked for a long, slow time, the binding may not be necessary. For a soup that has been cooked quickly, however, this is the step that really brings it together and gives the broth the long-cooked appearance. Another way to bind the soup is to spoon about a fourth of the beans into a blender, along with some broth, and purée it; then return to the soup.
6. Test soup for consistency. It should be thick, but not stiff. Add more water or stock if needed.

7. Test for flavour. If water has been used instead of a rich stock, you may need to add some tamari, yeast extract or powdered vegetable broth.
8. Finally, test for saltiness. When you taste it, the soup should say "Yes! That's right." If it doesn't, try adding some salt.
9. Serve at a temperature which is piping hot yet doesn't burn the tongue.
10. Top with chopped parsley, grated cheese, or croûtons. Serve with a hot grain or fresh bread, to complement the protein.

Emergency
If the soup isn't done, and everyone has arrived for dinner, put the whole lot in the blender, purée it, then very carefully cook for a few more minutes, stirring constantly to avoid burning. This soup isn't as lovely as the long-cooked one, but it will do in a pinch.

Variations
This recipe is the base for an endless number of variations. After the beans are cooked add tinned tomatoes, chopped carrots, spinach, kale (thinly cut with scissors), cauliflower or broccoli, etc. Use what you have on hand.
To complement the protein, during the last hour of cooking add rice or barley.
Leftover vegetables can be added towards the end.

Tofu Whey Soup

A light soup with an oriental flavour.

METRIC/IMPERIAL

110g/4oz leeks or spring onions

1 litre/2 pints whey from homemade tofu

1 Tbsp tamari (approximately)

110g/4oz tofu

Makes 4 servings

AMERICAN

1½ cups leeks or green onions

5 cups whey from homemade tofu

1½ Tbsp tamari (approximately)

¾ cup tofu

Makes 4 servings

1. Prepare leeks by making a slit in the side and washing out all dirt. Chop leeks in 1.5cm(½in) segments, including green part.
2. Bring whey to a boil. Add leeks, then simmer for 15 minutes, or until tender.
3. Add tamari to taste.
4. Cut tofu into bite-sized cubes, and add at the end, just to heat.

Variation
Use mushrooms instead of, or in addition to, leeks.

A Different Minestrone

With salad and fresh bread, a satisfying peasant's meal.

METRIC/IMPERIAL

Several vegetables in season (such as potatoes, carrots, courgettes, green beans, onions, cabbage, squash, etc.)

water or stock

½ onion per serving

olive oil

parmesan cheese (whole, if possible)

salt

1. Wash and chop vegetables.
2. In a soup pot, cover vegetables with water or stock and simmer until tender (about 30 minutes).
3. Meanwhile, slice onions in rings and quickly fry in olive oil until dark brown and crispy.
4. Grate cheese for topping.
5. When soup vegetables are tender, spoon about two-thirds into a blender; add some cooking water. Process until smooth.
6. Pour purée back into soup pot. Mix soup, and check consistency. Add more water if needed.
7. Taste for salt; add some if necessary.
8. Pour into individual soup bowls. Top with sautéed onions and grated cheese.

AMERICAN

Several vegetables in season (such as potatoes, carrots, courgettes, green beans, onions, cabbage, squash, etc.)

water or stock

½ onion per serving

olive oil

parmesan cheese (whole, if possible)

salt

Variation

For a non-dairy soup, substitute tamari roasted sunflower seeds for the cheese.

Cream of Celery

This is a rich, non-dairy soup.

METRIC/IMPERIAL

60g/2oz sunflower seeds, cashews or blanched almonds

225g/8oz celery and leaves

2 Tbsp oil, preferably corn oil

3 cups water

2 Tbsp flour

3 tsp tamari

1 tsp marjoram

Makes 4 servings

1. Wash and chop celery and leaves.
2. In a saucepan, sauté celery and leaves in oil.
3. When celery is beginning to become tender, add water, then simmer until tender.
4. Put sunflower seeds in blender with enough cooking water to cover and process until smooth.
5. Add celery, remaining cooking water and flour; blend for another minute, or until completely smooth.
6. For a very delicate soup, pass through a strainer.
7. Return to saucepan and simmer for five minutes, to allow flour to cook.
8. Add tamari and marjoram. Taste for saltiness and add more tamari if needed.

AMERICAN

½ cup sunflower seeds, cashews or blanched almonds

2½ cups chopped celery and leaves

2 Tbsp oil, preferably corn oil

3 cups water

2 Tbsp flour

3 tsp tamari

1 tsp marjoram

Makes 4 servings

Variation

Use any other vegetable in place of celery.

Caraway Seed Soup

A folk remedy—for winter, or for when you're out of sorts. It's presented in small quantity because this is the sort of soup you eat when you're alone, or that you make for someone who isn't feeling well.

METRIC/IMPERIAL

1 tsp. caraway seeds
1 Tbsp oil
1 Tbsp butter
2 Tbsp flour
½ litre/1 pint hot water
¼ tsp salt
handful of croûtons
parsley

Makes 2 servings

AMERICAN

1 tsp caraway seeds
1 Tbsp oil
1 Tbsp butter
2 Tbsp flour
2 cups hot water
¼ tsp salt
handful of croûtons
parsley

Makes 2 servings

1. In a small saucepan, heat oil and butter.
2. Add caraway seeds and stir them as they pop.
3. Mix in flour and cook over medium heat for about 3 minutes. Mixture should be dark, but not burned.
4. Slowly add hot water, while stirring. Bring to a boil.
5. Add salt. Taste, and add more salt if needed.
6. Top with croûtons and finely chopped parsley.

Garlic Soup

Good for what ails you.

METRIC/IMPERIAL

1 tsp caraway seeds
300g/10oz potatoes
1½ litres/2¾ pints water or stock
1 tsp salt
4 cloves garlic
1 Tbsp butter
croûtons

AMERICAN

1 tsp caraway seeds
2 cups chopped potatoes
7 cups water or stock
1 tsp salt
4 cloves garlic
1 Tbsp butter
croûtons

1. Crush caraway seeds with a mortar and pestle.
2. Wash and chop potatoes. Simmer potatoes with caraway seeds in salted water.
3. When potatoes are mushy, add crushed garlic and butter.
4. Serve with croûtons on top.

Potato Mushroom Soup

METRIC/IMPERIAL

500g/18oz potatoes

1½ litres/2¾ pints water or stock

100g/3½oz mixed vegetables (such as cabbage, celery, carrots, cauliflower, tomato)

1 Tbsp butter

100g/3½oz mushrooms

55g/2oz butter

30g/1oz flour

15g/½oz salt

1 clove garlic

1 tsp marjoram

parsley

Makes 6 servings

AMERICAN

3 cups chopped potatoes

7 cups water or stock

1 cup mixed vegetables (such as cabbage, celery, carrots, cauliflower, tomato)

1 Tbsp butter

2 cups sliced mushrooms

¼ cup butter

¼ cup flour

2½ tsp salt

1 clove garlic

1 tsp marjoram

parsley

Makes 6 servings

1. Wash and chop potatoes. In a soup pot, cook potatoes in boiling water or stock until almost soft.
2. Wash and chop vegetables. Sauté in 1 Tbsp butter until almost tender.
3. Brush or wipe mushrooms clean; slice and set aside.
4. In a small pan, melt butter; mix in flour and salt with a whisk. Cook over moderate heat for 5 minutes, stirring constantly. Whisk mixture into potato broth.
5. Add mushrooms and sautéed vegetables to potatoes and broth. Simmer for 25 minutes, stirring occasionally.
6. Just before serving, add crushed garlic and marjoram. Do not boil any more after that.
7. Serve topped with parsley.

Variations

Instead of marjoram, add pepper and paprika, or dill, or chives. Top soup with grated cheese.

Loren's Onion Soup

METRIC/IMPERIAL

680g/1½ lbs onions

1 medium carrot

1 tsp fresh grated ginger root

2 cloves garlic, minced

4-6 Tbsp butter or oil

1¼ litres/2 pints vegetable stock *or* water

tamari or miso to taste

Makes 4-6 servings

AMERICAN

8 cups onions

1 medium carrot

1 tsp fresh grated ginger root

2 cloves garlic, minced

¼-½ cup butter or oil

5 cups vegetable stock *or* water

tamari or miso to taste

Makes 4-6 servings

1. Peel onions; slice in thin crescents. (See vegetable chapter for illustrated instructions for slicing vegetables.)
2. Wash carrot and slice in matchsticks.
3. Fry fresh ginger and garlic in oil or butter. Add onions and carrots and fry lightly. As soon as vegetables are heated throughout, turn heat very low and continue cooking slowly, stirring occasionally, until onions are limp and completely tender (at least 30 minutes). If they have been cooked slowly enough, they will taste sweet.
4. Add stock and simmer for another 30 minutes.
5. Before serving, check the flavouring and add tamari or miso if needed for saltiness.

Variations

Add other vegetables, such as cauliflower or finely chopped kale.
For French onion soup, omit the carrots. Top each bowl with croûtons,
or with a round piece of toast. Sprinkle parmesan cheese on top and brown
under the grill (broiler). Top with a bit of chopped parsley.

Egyptian Red Lentil Soup

We received a shipment of lentils labelled 'Egyptian red lentils' so we named this soup after them. It is a quick and easy one.

METRIC/IMPERIAL

2 litres/4 pints water or stock

455g/1 lb red lentils

1 onion

2 Tbsp olive oil

4 Tbsp tamari (or less, if stock is used instead of water)

Makes 6 servings

AMERICAN

8 cups water or stock

2 cups red lentils

1 onion

2 Tbsp olive oil

¼ cup tamari (or less, if stock is used instead of water)

Makes 6 servings

1. Bring water to boil.
2. Add lentils and simmer until mushy. (About 30 minutes)
3. Meanwhile, slice onion in crescents and quickly sauté in oil until brown.
4. Add tamari to soup. Let cook for another couple of minutes. As tamaris differ in strength, it is necessary to taste soup to see if amount is right.
5. Stir in sautéed onions and serve. (If serving in individual bowls, ladle the soup in, then top with onions.)

White Bean Soup with Artichokes

METRIC/IMPERIAL

450g/1 lb haricot beans, or any white bean

1.7 litres/3 pints water

2 globe artichokes

8 cloves garlic

60g/2oz parsley, chopped fine

2 tsp basil

6 Tbsp olive oil

3 tsp salt

AMERICAN

2½ cups navy beans, or any white bean

2 quarts water

2 globe artichokes

8 cloves garlic

1 cup finely chopped parsley

2 tsp basil

½ cup olive oil

3 tsp salt

1. Wash and sort beans. Soak overnight in water.
2. Bring beans to a boil, then simmer for about one hour.
3. Meanwhile, prepare artichokes: cut into eighths and remove choke (whisker part in the middle) as well as the tougher outer leaves. Leave a good portion of the stem on. (Leftover outer leaves can be steamed separately for another meal.)
4. Add artichokes to the beans and continue simmering for another ½ hour, or just until beans are open and beginning to disintegrate, and artichokes are tender. Add more water, if needed, during cooking.
5. Make a paste of the peeled garlic, parsley, basil, olive oil and salt, by mashing well with a mortar and pestle. Add to soup at the very end of cooking, to preserve the fresh flavour of the seasonings.
6. Check consistency of soup. Add more water if needed. Taste, and add salt if needed.

Preparing Vegetables

The more food your body absorbs from the garden, the better.
As you eat, try always to think of all those who have helped with
the growing of the foodstuffs, the devas, the nature spirits, the
angels; by doing this you are showing your recognition and
appreciation for all that has been done to help the things grow here.

Eileen's guidance

I n vegetarian cooking, vegetables as a side dish often take a
more simple form because the main dish may be somewhat
complicated, and another complicated dish would detract from
the overall effect.

In cooking vegetables we wish to enhance, rather than disguise,
their natural flavour and beauty.

In order to enhance natural flavour and beauty, those qualities
must be there to begin with, which means that the vegetables must
be fresh. A teacher of mine once said rather vehemently,
"You modern cooks have it all backwards. You
look in a recipe book for what you want to
cook, make a list of ingredients, then go to
the market and buy them. It should be the
other way around. First go to the market
and see what vegetables call out to you
because of their beauty and freshness.
Take them home and figure out
what to do with them." This is
a tricky matter in these times,
because of cosmetic agriculture.
Often the largest and most colourful
vegetables are only so because of being
grown with chemicals, being dyed, waxed;
their taste and vitality is disappointing.
So have a discerning eye. Grow vegetables
yourself if possible; and if that is not possible
buy ones that have been grown by natural methods. And if you
must use the ordinary commercial vegetables, know that the
love and joy you put into their preparation can improve their
quality tremendously.

When you prepare vegetables, take enough time to allow a relationship to develop between you and them. Their strength and their beauty, as well as their life force, flow into you as you prepare them, if you are open to that. And as you become more sensitive to their form and grace, new ways of preparing the vegetables suggest themselves to you.

If possible, harvest vegetables immediately before preparing. If vegetables must be stored for a while, refrigerate them in an air-tight container or bag, so that their subtle flavour is protected from other surrounding flavours.

Wash vegetables quickly, and dry immediately afterwards. As many vitamins are water soluble, it is a good idea that vegetables have as little contact with water as possible.

Vegetable Cutting

A simple dish takes on a special feeling when extra care has been taken in cutting the vegetables.

Carrots can be cut diagonally, to reveal more of the inner pattern. The diagonal cuts can then be piled up and cut again, to form small matchsticks.

Celery butterflies are made by cutting the vegetable diagonally.

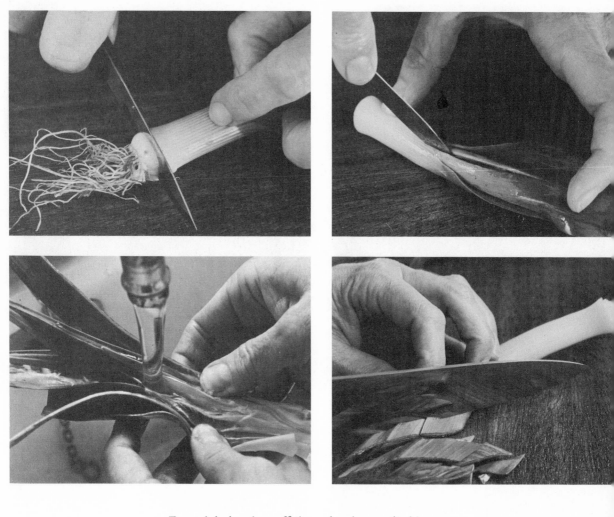

To wash leeks, chop off the end and any wilted leaves; then make a lengthwise slit in the leek, using the point of a small knife. Wash out all dirt trapped inside.

Cut leeks diagonally.

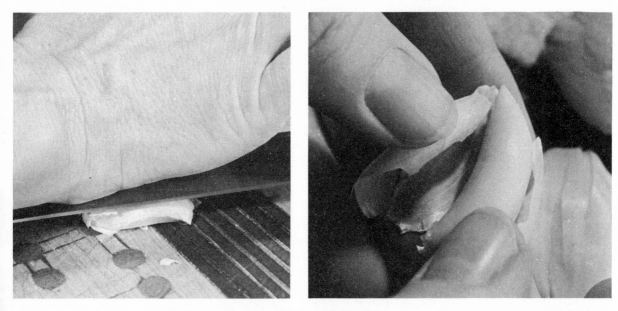

Garlic cloves can be peeled more quickly if each clove is
first given a blow with the side of a knife.

This releases the skin.

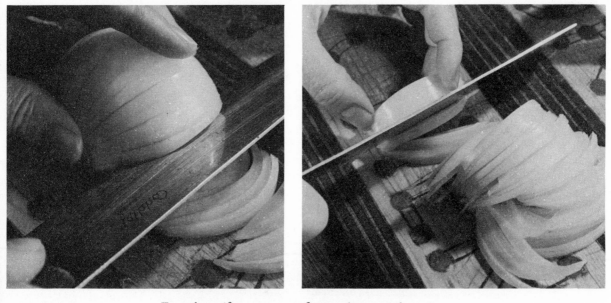

To make uniform crescents from onions, cut the onion
in half, then begin slicing next to the cutting board and
follow the growth lines in the onion right around.

Cooking Methods

Steaming:

The most satisfactory method for cooking most vegetables is to steam them. This method preserves the natural flavour and nutrients. If you don't have a steamer pot, small stainless steel steamers which fit inside a regular saucepan are available at most whole food shops. Put a small amount of water in a saucepan, wait for it to boil, then put in steamer with the vegetables in it. Cover and cook until vegetables are tender. For variety in flavour, after steaming toss vegetables in butter, tamari or fresh, chopped herbs.

Baking:

We're all accustomed to baking potatoes, but have you tried baking beetroot(beets), onions or winter squash?

Beetroot—Preheat oven to 220°C/Gas Mark 7/425°F. Wash beetroot and cut off their scrubby ends, but leave peels on. Place in baking dish and bake for 1-1½ hours (depending on their size). They are done when they can be easily pierced with a skewer. Serve with peels still on. They are crackly and sweet-tasting.

Onions—Preheat oven to 190°C/Gas Mark 5/375°F. Wash onions, but leave whole with the skins on. Bake in a baking dish for 1½ hours, or until they can be pierced with a skewer. To serve, remove skins by cutting off the end to which all the skin is attached and popping the onion out by pressing the skin. Serve with melted butter over them, or sautéed mushrooms. Garnish with chopped parsley.

Winter Squash — (This section is for Americans; I have not seen winter squash in Britain.) Butternut or acorn squash is ideal. Wash and dry the squash. Bake it whole at 375°F for at least 1 to 1½ hours, or until it can be pierced easily with a toothpick. When squash is done, remove it from the oven and split in half lengthwise. Scoop the strings and seeds from inside. Serve filled with melted butter and parsley, or with mushrooms sautéed in butter and garlic.

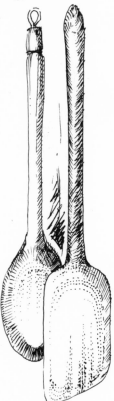

Baked Potatoes — For an easy, satisfying main dish, top baked potatoes with grated cheese, yogurt or soured cream, chopped chives and sautéed vegetables, such as mushrooms, green peppers, onions, courgettes, etc.

Sautéing à la Michael Worth:

This is especially good with cabbage, curly kale or other greens. Wash greens and chop, leaving water on leaves. Melt butter in a large saucepan, then add greens and stir while frying until butter is distributed evenly. Cover saucepan, lower heat and steam-fry until greens are tender, stirring occasionally so that they don't burn. Add caraway seeds or herbs at the end. (Michael adds beer or turmeric to everything, but I wouldn't advise it.)

Stir-Frying:

To make the optimum use of fuel when it was scarce, the Chinese developed the method of stir-frying. Because the vegetables are cut very thin and are cooked by a combination of oil and steam, they are done very quickly. The valuable nutrients in the cooking water are consumed, because the water is thickened into a sauce. Although the classic seasoning for a stir-fried dish is garlic and ginger, other seasonings can be used as well. (A good dish is fried matchstick carrots, seasoned with cumin.)

The proper pan to use for stir-frying is a wok with a lid. If you don't have one, use a large frying pan, or a saucepan, preferably with rounded corners.

Vegetables that are particularly good in stir-fried dishes are long mung bean sprouts, snow peas, celery and mushrooms.

When vegetables are cooked and sauce is finished, roasted cashews or roasted blanched almonds can be added. Cubed tofu is also very appropriate, and must be added at the end, so that the tofu is not broken up too much in the stir-frying.

The method used in the following pages can be altered by using salt instead of tamari. In this case the sauce will be white instead of brown.

Stir Frying

1. Choose several vegetables which offer a variety of colour and texture. Vegetables often used in stir-fried dishes are snow peas, mung bean sprouts, mushrooms and celery.
2. Slice all vegetables very thin, then arrange on a plate or in separate bowls. Place together vegetables which take the same cooking time. Carrots and onions, for example, cook in about the same time, but mushrooms cook very quickly, so they will be kept apart and added at the end.
3. Finely chop garlic and grate ginger. Use 1 tsp of each for a small amount of vegetables.
4. Mix 2-8 Tbsp cornflour (cornstarch) or arrowroot with a small amount of cold water.
5. Have easily available garlic, ginger, vegetables, oil, tamari, water and cornflour mixture.
6. Put wok over high heat.
7. When it is hot add small amount of oil, and the garlic and ginger.
8. Add longer-cooking vegetables.
9. Quickly flip them around, to sear in the flavour.
10. Add a small amount of water.

3

5

8

39

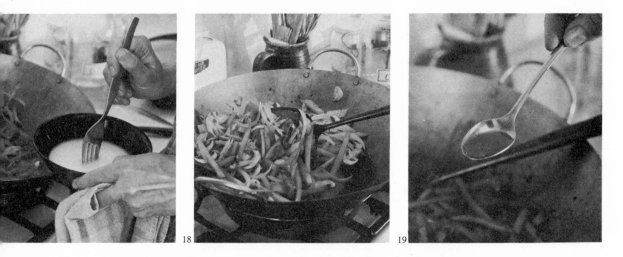

18 19

11. Quickly cover the wok. Cook vegetables for a few minutes. Lower the heat if it sounds as though they are cooking so rapidly that they might burn.
12. Add remaining vegetables. The timing on this depends on what vegetables you have used and how thinly you have cut them. But estimate the difference in cooking time between longer-cooking and quickly-cooking vegetables, and add them so that all will be done simultaneously.
13. Mix vegetables in and replace cover.
14. Let vegetables continue to cook until they are crunchy done. The best way to test is to bite into a couple of them.
15. The next three steps must be done very quickly, so that vegetables neither burn nor overcook. Tilt wok so that cooking liquid all runs to one side. Add tamari to taste.
16. Give cornflour and water another little stir.
17. Then combine with cooking liquid.
18. Quickly stir sauce into vegetables, scooping under them to coat thoroughly. Sauce should be thickened just enough to cling to vegetables.
19. Taste sauce and add more tamari if needed, then more thickener if needed.

Serve  immediately.

Main Course Savouries

Your attitude when you eat anything
should be one of joy and pleasure and thanksgiving.
You are to be constantly aware that all these gifts are Mine.

Eileen's guidance

Vegetarian cookery does not strictly adhere to the traditional classifications of main and side dishes. Often a very hearty soup or a salad serves as an entire meal. In other cases several vegetable dishes combine to make the main course. So, although the following are suggestions for 'main course savouries', remember that you can use 'main' and 'side' dishes almost interchangeably. In this way, cooking with vegetables is infinitely versatile, as we combine and recombine to create whole and satisfying meals.

The Simplest Supper

METRIC/IMPERIAL

185g/6½oz millet

570ml/1 pint milk

½ tsp salt

2 onions

2 Tbsp oil

1 head cabbage

Makes 4 servings

AMERICAN

1 cup millet

2½ cups milk

½ tsp salt

2 onions

2 Tbsp oil

1 head cabbage

Makes 4 servings

1. In a bowl, cover millet with boiling water. Wash around a bit, then drain. Repeat this procedure. (This hastens cooking of millet, and washes the grain as well.)
2. Bring milk to a boil. Add drained millet and salt; simmer for 20 minutes, or until tender.
3. Peel and chop onions. Sauté in oil until crispy and brown and very sweet-tasting.
4. Wash cabbage. Cut into fourths and remove hard core. Chop cabbage into bite-sized pieces, then steam.
5. To serve, put a spoonful of cabbage on each plate, and a spoonful of millet topped with sautéed onions.

Cauliflower Cheese

This is probably the single most popular dish in our community — possibly because it's so easy that nearly everyone can make it; and it tastes wonderful.

METRIC/IMPERIAL

510g/1½ lbs cauliflower, weighed without leaves

60g/2oz butter

4 Tbsp flour

½ tsp salt

½ tsp dry mustard

½ litre/1 pint milk, *or* half milk and half cauliflower cooking water

225g/8oz cheddar cheese, grated

paprika

Makes 4 servings

AMERICAN

1 large cauliflower

4 Tbsp butter

4 Tbsp flour

½ tsp salt

½ tsp dry mustard

2 cups milk, *or* half milk and half cauliflower cooking water

2 cups grated cheddar cheese

paprika

Makes 4 servings

1. Preheat oven to 190°C/Gas Mark 5/375°F.
2. Wash cauliflower and break into flowerettes. Steam until not quite tender. Drain, reserving cooking water.
3. In a saucepan melt butter, then mix in flour, salt and mustard; slowly cook for at least 5 minutes, stirring constantly.
4. Gradually add liquid, stirring all the while; cook until mixture thickens. (Using cooking water instead of half of the milk gives the dish more of the cauliflower flavour.)
5. When sauce has thickened, add grated cheese and stir until melted.
6. Place cauliflower in greased baking dish and pour sauce over it.
7. Bake for 30 minutes or until sauce is bubbly and browned on top.

Mushroom Stuffed Peppers

METRIC/IMPERIAL

3 large red bell peppers

225g/8oz fresh mushrooms

2 Tbsp chopped parsley

1oz Jerusalem artichokes

85g/3oz Gouda cheese

3oz butter

1oz onion, finely chopped

1½oz plain flour

½ tsp dry mustard

½ tsp salt

340ml/12fl oz soured cream

Makes 6 servings

1. Bring water to boil in a saucepan.
2. Cut peppers in half lengthwise. Remove stems and seeds. Drop into boiling water and cook, uncovered, for 4 minutes. Remove from water and allow to drain in a colander.
3. Brush or wipe mushrooms clean; then slice.
4. Chop parsley; slice Jerusalem artichokes.
5. Grate cheese.
6. Chop onions.
7. Melt part of the butter in a saucepan, then sautē onions until translucent.
8. Add remaining butter; then blend in flour, mustard and salt; cook over low heat for five minutes, stirring constantly.
9. Still stirring, blend in soured cream and cook until mixture thickens.
10. Remove from heat and add parsley, Jerusalem artichokes and sliced mushrooms.
11. Pile filling into pepper halves. Sprinkle grated cheese over top.
12. Place under grill (broiler) for about 5 minutes, or place on top rack in a very hot oven. Cook until cheese is bubbly. Serve immediately.

AMERICAN

3 large red bell peppers

½ lb fresh mushrooms

2 Tbsp chopped parsley

¼ cup Jerusalem artichokes

¾ cup grated jack cheese

6 Tbsp butter

¼ cup finely chopped onion

6 Tbsp white flour

½ tsp dry mustard

½ tsp salt

1½ cups sour cream

Makes 6 servings

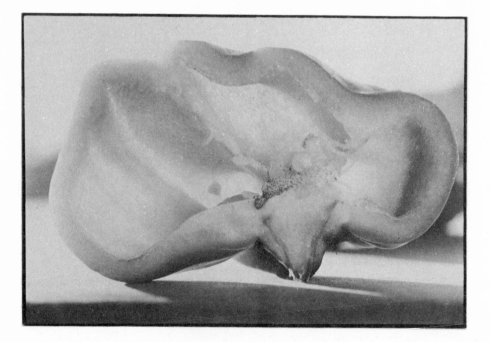

Heroic Cheese Soufflé

METRIC/IMPERIAL

40g/1½oz butter

3 Tbsp flour

¼ tsp salt

½ tsp mustard powder

⅛ tsp cayenne

225ml/8fl oz milk

225g/8oz cheddar cheese, grated

6 egg whites

6 egg yolks

Makes 4-6 servings

AMERICAN

3 Tbsp butter

3 Tbsp flour

¼ tsp salt

½ tsp mustard powder

⅛ tsp cayenne

1 cup milk

2 cups grated cheddar cheese

6 egg whites

6 egg yolks

Makes 4-6 servings

Dedicated to Sir George Trevelyan,
who gave the dish its name.

1. Melt butter in a saucepan. With a whisk, blend in flour until completely smooth. Add salt, mustard powder and cayenne; cook over low heat for at least 5 minutes, stirring all the while.
2. Turn heat up to moderate and, continuing to stir mixture with a whisk, slowly add milk. When sauce has thickened and is just beginning to bubble, remove from heat.
3. Add grated cheese and stir until cheese has melted. Let sauce cool.
4. Preheat oven to 180°C/Gas Mark 4/350°F.
5. Beat egg whites until stiff. Set aside.
6. Beat egg yolks slightly and add to cheese sauce, mixing thoroughly.
7. Barely fold egg whites into cheese mixture, using hands or a spatula. The lightness of the soufflé depends on the whites not being broken up very much.
8. Liberally rub the bottom and sides of a straight-sided baking dish with butter, then dust with flour. Try your various baking dishes until you find one that the soufflé fills at least ¾ full. As it bakes the soufflé will expand and create a golden puff rising out of the dish; hence its heroic quality.
9. Spoon mixture into baking dish; bake for 40 minutes or until soufflé is set and a knife inserted comes out clean.

Tofu Teriyaki

METRIC/IMPERIAL

1 kg/2 lbs tofu

2 tsp grated fresh
ginger

5 cloves garlic

2 Tbsp oil

½ tsp dry mustard

110ml/4fl oz apple
juice concentrate

110ml/4fl oz tamari

¼ litre/½ pint water

2 Tbsp arrowroot
(approximately)

4 Tbsp cold water

parsley

Makes 6 servings

1. Cut tofu into individual serving-sized slices, and drain;
   arrange in one layer in a glass baking dish.
2. In a blender place ginger, garlic, oil, mustard and apple
   concentrate. Blend until completely smooth; then add
   tamari and water and blend for a few more seconds.
3. Pour sauce over tofu; marinate for 2 hours.
4. Preheat oven to 210°C/Gas Mark 6/400°F.
5. Bake tofu in marinade for 20 minutes, or until piping hot.
6. Carefully remove tofu to a hot serving platter. Put platter
   in warm oven while sauce is being finished.
7. Pour sauce out of baking dish into a saucepan.
8. Dissolve arrowroot in cold water, then whisk into sauce
   as it heats. The correct amount of arrowroot varies,
   depending on how much liquid has been lost in the
   cooking, so add gradually until thickness suits your taste.
   Note: Arrowroot does not need to be cooked, as does
   cornflour or flour, so as soon as it thickens sauce may
   be served.
9. Pour sauce over tofu; garnish with parsley.

Note:
Various brands of apple juice concentrate and tamari differ in
strength, so the flavour of this sauce may change each time.
you change brands. Therefore, to preserve the sweet-salt
balance, add more concentrate or tamari as needed.

AMERICAN

2 lbs tofu

2½ tsp grated
fresh ginger

5 cloves garlic

2½ Tbsp oil

½ tsp dry mustard

½ cup apple juice
concentrate

½ cup tamari

1 cup water

2 Tbsp arrowroot
(approximately)

4 Tbsp cold water

parsley

Makes 6 servings

Moussaka

METRIC/IMPERIAL

1.25kg/3 lb aubergines

salt

olive oil

110g/4oz walnuts, ground

30g/1oz bread crumbs

30g/1oz wheat germ

¼ tsp pepper

1 egg

4 Tbsp milk

2 onions

170g/6oz mushrooms

6 Tbsp tomato paste

1 tsp cinnamon

4 Tbsp water

30g/1oz chopped parsley

60g/2oz butter

4 Tbsp flour

½ tsp nutmeg

¼ tsp salt

½ litre/1 pint milk

2 egg yolks

4 Tbsp parmesan cheese

Makes 10 servings

AMERICAN

3 lbs eggplant

salt

olive oil

1 cup ground walnuts

4 Tbsp bread crumbs

¼ cup wheat germ

¼ tsp pepper

1 egg

4 Tbsp milk

2 onions

2 cups sliced mushrooms

6 Tbsp tomato paste

1 tsp cinnamon

4 Tbsp water

½ cup chopped parsley

4 Tbsp butter

4 Tbsp flour

½ tsp nutmeg

¼ tsp salt

2 cups milk

2 egg yolks

4 Tbsp parmesan cheese

Makes 10 servings

1. Peel and slice aubergines (eggplant). Sprinkle with salt. Allow bitter juices to drain for at least ½ hour. Pat aubergines dry.
2. Fry aubergine slices in olive oil. Drain.
3. Mix together walnuts, bread crumbs, wheat germ, pepper, egg and milk. Mixture should be moist.
4. Chop onions and mushrooms. Fry onions in oil and, when translucent, add mushrooms and continue frying until mushrooms are just tender.
5. To onions and mushrooms add nut mixture, tomato paste and cinnamon. Add water and cook over low heat for 10 minutes, stirring often. Add parsley.
6. Preheat oven to 190°C/Gas Mark 5/375°F.
7. Place alternate layers of aubergine and nut mixture in a greased baking dish, beginning and ending with aubergine.
8. Melt butter in a saucepan. Blend in flour, nutmeg and salt; then cook over a low heat for 5 minutes, stirring constantly. Blend in milk with a whisk, and cook over moderate heat, still stirring, until sauce thickens. Beat egg yolks in a bowl; mix a little of the sauce with yolks, then return mixture to sauce. Heat slightly but do not boil.
9. Pour sauce over aubergine layers.
10. Top with grated parmesan cheese.
11. Bake for 45 minutes, or until bubbly and browned on top.

Mama Imperatore's Italian Tomato Sauce

Make this sauce in large quantity, then freeze part of it.

METRIC/IMPERIAL

1 bulb garlic

5-8 onions

olive oil

4 bay leaves

2 tsp basil

2 tsp oregano

2.6kg/5 lb 12oz tinned whole tomatoes

425g/15oz tomato paste

¼ litre/½ pint red wine

3 tsp salt

¼ tsp pepper

pinch of bicarbonate of soda (cuts acidity)

Makes 25 servings:
3 litres/5 pints/
12½ cups

AMERICAN

1 bulb garlic

5-8 onions

olive oil

4 bay leaves

2 tsp basil

2 tsp oregano

5 lb 12oz canned whole tomatoes

15oz tomato paste

1 cup red wine

3 tsp salt

¼ tsp pepper

pinch of baking soda (cuts acidity)

Makes 25 servings:
12½ cups

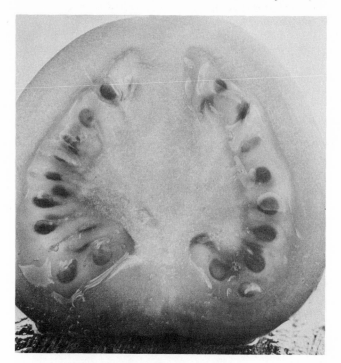

1. Separate garlic bulb into cloves; peel and finely mince.
2. Peel and chop onions.
3. In a large soup pot; sauté garlic, onions and herbs in oil.
4. Remove top from tomato tin, but leave contents in tin and cut tomatoes up by slicing through them several times with a knife.
5. Add tomatoes and tomato paste to onion mixture, as well as wine, salt and pepper, and soda.
6. Bring sauce to a boil, then reduce heat and simmer *very* slowly for at least 10 hours. Put asbestos pad or flame spreader between the pot and the heat; or, better yet, cook sauce in a crock pot (slow cooker) or on the slow section of an Aga or a wood stove. Check sauce occasionally to see that it isn't cooking too rapidly; add water if needed. Pot should be covered.
7. For the last two hours of cooking remove the lid, so that sauce can reduce and turn darker.
8. Serve sauce over pasta or polenta; or use in lasagne.

Vegetable Plait

A way to make very common ingredients seem special.

Metric/Imperial

Makes 8 servings

METRIC/IMPERIAL

Filling: Pt. I

110g/4oz celery
340g/12oz potatoes
270g/9½oz carrots
140g/5oz parsnips
140g/5oz swede
140g/5oz green peas

Sauce

1 onion
4 cloves
1 bay leaf
570ml/1 pint milk
60g/2oz butter
60g/2oz flour
½ tsp salt
15g/½oz cheese, grated

Filling: Pt. II

2 onions
oil
110g/4oz cheese, grated

Makes 8 servings

AMERICAN

Filling: Pt. I

1 cup celery
2 cups potatoes
2 cups carrots
1 cup parsnips
1 cup swede (rutabaga)
2 cups green peas

Sauce

1 onion
4 cloves
1 bay leaf
2½ cups milk
¼ cup butter
¼ cup flour
½ tsp salt
2 Tbsp grated cheese

Filling: Pt. II

2 onions
oil
1 cup grated cheese

Filling: Pt. I

1. Wash and dice celery, potatoes, carrots, parsnips and swedes in 1cm(½in) cubes. Leave peas whole.
2. Steam each vegetable separately until just tender. Do not allow to get mushy. If peas are frozen, just thaw, do not cook.
3. Drain vegetables well.

Sauce

1. With a knife make 6-8 slits in onion. Stud onion with cloves; insert a bay leaf in one of the slits.
2. Slowly heat milk for 15 minutes, with onion in it. Let milk cool slightly.
3. In a separate saucepan, whisk flour into melted butter, then cook for at least 5 minutes over medium heat, stirring constantly.
4. Slowly add milk through a strainer, while continuing to stir. Cook until sauce thickens; simmer, covered, for 15 minutes.
5. Stir in grated cheese until melted.

Filling: Pt. II

1. Dice onions and fry in oil until golden brown.
2. Grate cheese.

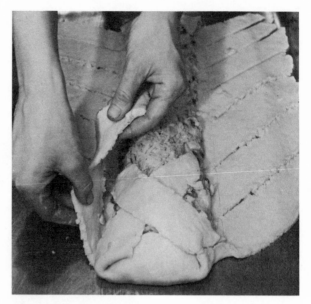

Pastry

225g/8oz plain flour

½ tsp salt

100g/3½oz margarine

3 Tbsp ice cold water

1 egg

1 Tbsp water or milk

Gravy

2 onions

30g/1oz butter

2 Tbsp flour

570ml/1 pint stock

parsley for garnish

Pastry

1. Combine flour and salt; then work in margarine until texture of bread crumbs.
2. Add enough ice water that pastry can be gathered up in a ball.

Gravy

1. Slice onions in thin crescents.
2. Melt butter in a saucepan, then very slowly fry onions for ½ hour.
3. Stir flour in thoroughly, and continue cooking for at least 5 minutes.
4. Whisk in the stock. Increase heat and continue stirring until gravy thickens.
5. Add salt, if needed. If water has been used instead of stock, add a bit of tamari, Marmite, yeast extract or powdered vegetable broth to give flavour to the gravy.

Assembly

1. Preheat oven to 190°C/Gas Mark 5/375°F.
2. Mix vegetables with enough sauce to hold them together, without being sloppy.
3. On a floured surface, roll pastry into the largest rectangle possible.
4. At Findhorn we have very large baking pans and ovens, so we can put the whole pastry inside the pan. However, as you will probably be using a smaller pan and oven, fold the pastry in half, then carefully lift and unfold it over a flat baking tin, placing it so that the central part of the pastry is on the tin; the edges can extend beyond it, because they will eventually be folded over anyway.

Pastry

2 cups white flour

½ tsp salt

7 Tbsp margarine

3 Tbsp ice cold water

1 egg

1 Tbsp water or milk

Gravy

2 onions

2 Tbsp butter

2 Tbsp flour

2½ cups stock

parsley for garnish

5. Cut pastry as shown in photograph; strips should be about 2.5cm (1 inch) wide. There must be an equal number of wings on each side.
6. Spoon vegetable-sauce mixture into pastry, as neatly as possible. The sides of the filling should slope in toward the top, and the filling should not extend to the part of the pastry which has been cut.
7. Sprinkle fried onions, then grated cheese over filling.
8. Plait (braid) pastry as shown in photograph. Begin with the 'point' end of the arrow. Fold 'point' over filling, then alternate folding left and right wings over filling.
Before reaching opposite end, fold end piece over filling.
9. Beat an egg with 1 Tbsp water or milk, and brush pastry with beaten egg.
10. Bake for ½ hour, or until nicely browned.

To Serve carefully remove plait to a serving platter. This will require two people and several spatulas. Garnish plait with parsley. Serve gravy in a separate dish. Slice plait for individual servings, and pour gravy over.

Variations
The vegetables we have used in the filling reflect middle-of-the-winter conditions in Scotland. Many other vegetables can be used in place of the predominantly root vegetables.
Also, instead of using a variety of vegetables, a single one can be used, such as spinach or mushrooms.

Polenta

170g/6oz polenta or maize meal

¼ litre/½ pint cold water

1 tsp salt

½ litre/1 pint boiling water

110g/4oz cheese, grated

½ litre/1 pint Italian tomato sauce (see page 50)

Makes 4 servings

1. Stir together polenta, cold water and salt.
2. Bring water to boil in heavy saucepan or top of double saucepan. Add polenta mixture, stirring constantly.
3. Bring to boil, then simmer, stirring constantly, until thickened.
4. Preheat oven to 180°C/Gas Mark 4/350°F.
5. Rub a baking dish with butter.
6. Spoon in half the polenta, then sprinkle a layer of grated cheese, saving a little cheese for the top; then cover with remaining polenta and sprinkle with cheese.
7. Bake for ½ hour. Meanwhile heat the sauce.
8. Remove polenta from oven when done and let set for 5 minutes. Then slice in squares. Serve with sauce spooned over.

Variation
Slice ½ lb mushrooms into tomato sauce while heating.

1 cup polenta or corn meal

1 cup cold water

1 tsp salt

2 cups boiling water

1 cup grated cheese

2 cups Italian tomato sauce (see page 50)

Makes 4 servings

Spinach Dumplings

225g/8oz spinach

85g/3oz dry bread

85g/3oz cheddar cheese

2 eggs

¼ tsp garlic powder

30g/1oz parmesan cheese, grated

salt and pepper

flour

½ litre/1 pint Italian tomato sauce (see page 50)

15g/½oz parmesan cheese

Makes 4 servings

Make these dumplings when you have some time the night before.

1. Wash spinach, and steam until tender. Drain.
2. Chop together (preferably in a blender or food grinder) the spinach, bread and cheese.
3. Beat eggs well and add to spinach mixture.
4. Add garlic powder, parmesan cheese, and salt and pepper to taste. Mix well.
5. Put mixture in a covered container, and refrigerate for at least 3 hours or overnight.
6. Roll spoonfuls of the mixture into small balls. Dip in flour; place on a plate.
7. Preheat oven to 190°C/Gas Mark 5/375°F.
8. Drop dumplings into boiling salted water. Cook until they float to the top (about 1 minute). Remove with tea strainer or slotted spoon. Drain.
9. Place dumplings in a greased casserole dish and cover with tomato sauce. Sprinkle with parmesan cheese; bake until bubbly.

Suggestion
Serve with pasta.

8oz spinach (1 cup cooked)

2 slices dry bread

¾ cup grated cheddar cheese

2 eggs

¼ tsp garlic powder

¼ cup grated parmesan cheese

salt and pepper

flour

2½ cups Italian tomato sauce (see page 50)

2 Tbsp parmesan cheese

Makes 4 servings

Lasagne

METRIC/IMPERIAL

340g/12oz lasagne noodles

½ litre/1 pint Italian tomato sauce

110g/4oz mozzarella cheese (or edam)

170g/6oz ricotta cheese (or cottage cheese)

1 egg

225g/8oz spinach

110g/4oz mushrooms

30g/1oz butter

2 Tbsp flour

¼ litre/½ pint milk

¼ tsp nutmeg

¼ tsp salt

30g/1oz parmesan cheese, grated

30g/1oz bread crumbs

Makes 6 servings

AMERICAN

12oz lasagne noodles

2½ cups Italian tomato sauce

1 cup grated mozzarella cheese

¾ cup ricotta cheese

1 egg

½ lb spinach

2 cups sliced mushrooms

2 Tbsp butter

2 Tbsp flour

1 cup milk

¼ tsp nutmeg

¼ tsp salt

¼ cup grated parmesan cheese

¼ cup bread crumbs

Makes 6 servings

1. Drop lasagne noodles into boiling salted water one by one, and stir after each addition.
2. When noodles are not quite tender, remove from water one by one and lay on towel to drain.
3. Grate mozzarella cheese; combine with ricotta and beaten egg. Set aside.
4. Steam spinach until almost tender. Drain, then chop into large pieces.
5. Brush or wipe mushrooms clean. Slice.
6. Make béchamel sauce: in a saucepan, add flour to melted butter and cook for 5 minutes, stirring constantly. Increase heat and continue stirring while slowly adding milk. When sauce thickens, add nutmeg and salt. Remove from heat and stir in spinach and mushrooms.
7. Mix together parmesan cheese and bread crumbs.
8. To assemble lasagne: rub a large flat baking dish with butter, then lay one layer of noodles on bottom, followed by layer of one half of the tomato sauce, then noodles, ricotta mixture, noodles, béchamel sauce mixture, noodles, remaining tomato sauce, parmesan cheese and bread crumbs.
9. Bake at 180°C/Gas Mark 4/350°F for one hour, or until bubbly.

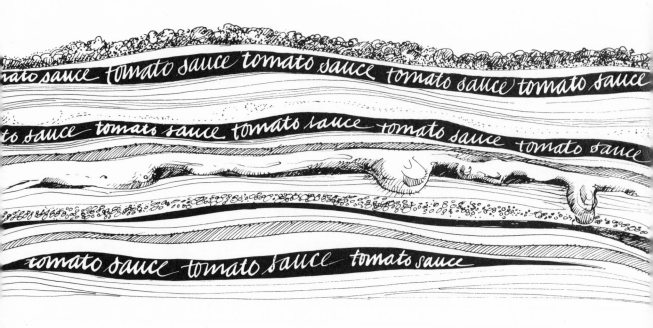

Leek & Mushroom Quiche

Pastry

40g/1½ oz rolled oats

55g/2oz soft wholemeal flour

30g/1oz sesame seeds

½ tsp salt

¼ tsp dry mustard

30g/1oz cheese, grated

70g/2½oz butter

2 Tbsp water

Filling

200g/7oz leeks

110g/4oz mushrooms

55g/2oz cheese, grated

parsley

455ml/16fl oz milk

3 eggs

¼ tsp salt

nutmeg

Makes 6 servings

Pastry

½ cup rolled oats

½ cup whole wheat pastry flour

¼ cup sesame seeds

½ tsp salt

¼ tsp dry mustard

¼ cup grated cheese

⅓ cup butter

2 Tbsp water

Filling

2 cups chopped leeks

2 cups sliced mushrooms

½ cup grated cheese

parsley

2 cups milk

3 eggs

¼ tsp salt

nutmeg

Makes 6 servings

Pastry

1. Mix together the oats, flour, seeds, salt, mustard and grated cheese.
2. Cut in butter until well blended.
3. Add as much water as needed to hold pastry together.
4. With fingers press dough into a 23cm(9in) round pie tin. If you wish, refrigerate dough, in the tin, for an hour or more before baking.
5. Preheat oven to 220°C/Gas Mark 7/425°F.
6. Bake pastry for 15 minutes, or until browned. Remove from oven.

Filling

The filling can be started while pastry is being refrigerated, or as the pastry is baking.

1. Prepare leeks by making a lengthwise slit with a knife, and thoroughly washing out any dirt that might be trapped inside. Remove any wilted parts, then chop leeks into 2cm(¾in) segments.
2. Steam leeks until tender. Drain thoroughly.
3. Brush or wipe mushrooms clean, then slice.
4. Grate cheese and chop parsley very fine.
5. To shorten cooking time of quiche, scald the milk.
6. Beat eggs and salt, and combine with milk, mixing thoroughly.
7. Line bottom of pastry with leeks, followed by raw mushrooms, cheese and parsley. Pour egg-milk mixture over all. Sprinkle a bit of nutmeg on top.
8. Bake at 190°C/Gas Mark 5/375°F for 35 to 40 minutes, or until quiche is set and a knife inserted in the centre comes out clean.

Variations

For a more delicate quiche, use shortcrust pastry. (Recipe appears in *Desserts* section).

In place of leeks and mushrooms, substitute any fresh vegetable in season.

Slice the vegetable very thin, then lightly sauté or steam.

Allow vegetables to drain completely before adding to the quiche.

For snacks or appetisers, make individual quiches in muffin tins.

Loaf & Gravy

This is a dish that non-vegetarians find very satisfying.

METRIC/IMPERIAL

140g/5oz green lentils

½ tsp sage

140g/5oz brown rice

140g/5oz millet

1 onion

1 carrot

2 stalks celery and leaves

2 Tbsp oil

30g/1oz maize meal

30g/1oz almonds or cashews, chopped

½ tsp thyme

½ tsp salt

1 Tbsp tamari

15g/½oz fresh parsley, chopped fine

Gravy

1 onion

2 Tbsp oil

225g/8oz mushrooms (very ripe mushrooms give more flavour)

570ml/1 pint water

½ tsp basil

1 bay leaf

6 Tbsp cornflour or arrowroot

110ml/4fl oz cold water

3-5 Tbsp tamari

Makes 10 servings

AMERICAN

¾ cup lentils

½ tsp sage

¾ cup brown rice

¾ cup millet

1 onion

1 carrot

2 stalks celery and leaves

2 Tbsp oil

¼ cup corn meal

¼ cup chopped almonds or cashews

½ tsp thyme

½ tsp salt

1 Tbsp tamari

2 Tbsp chopped fresh parsley

Gravy

1 onion

2 Tbsp oil

2 cups sliced mushrooms (very ripe mushrooms give more flavour)

2½ cups water

½ tsp basil

1 bay leaf

¼ cup cornstarch or arrowroot

½ cup cold water

3-5 Tbsp tamari

Makes 10 servings

Loaf

1. Cook lentils with sage in unsalted water. When done, drain and save excess water.
2. Cook rice and millet together in unsalted water.
3. Wash and chop onions, carrot and celery. Sauté in oil until tender.
4. Preheat oven to 180°C/Gas Mark 4/350°F.
5. In a large bowl, or with an electric mixer, combine all loaf ingredients. Mixture should hold together in a ball, but not be dry. Add lentils' cooking water if needed to moisten mixture. Emergency note: If you've let the mixture get too wet, that can be remedied by adding more maize meal (corn meal).
6. Taste for saltiness and add tamari if needed.
7. Place in oiled loaf pan. Bake for one hour.
8. Serve in slices, with gravy spooned over.

Gravy

1. Slice onions in thin crescents. (see *Preparing Vegetables* for instructions.) Sauté onions in oil.
2. Clean mushrooms with a brush or a cloth (do not wash them, as they absorb too much water). Slice mushrooms.
3. When onions are translucent, add mushrooms and continue cooking briefly until mushrooms are tender.
4. Add water, basil and bay leaf. Bring to a boil, then reduce heat to simmer.
5. Mix cornflour (cornstarch) and cold water together until completely smooth. Slowly add to simmering gravy, stirring constantly, until gravy thickens to your liking.
6. Add tamari to taste. This is a thick, hearty gravy, reminiscent of non-vegetarian gravies. As tamaris differ in strength, it is necessary to add a little bit at a time, tasting all the while.
7. Let sauce simmer very gently, covered, for 20 minutes.

Peter's Omelette

METRIC/IMPERIAL

3 eggs
⅛ tsp salt
pinch of pepper
butter
filling

Makes one omelette

AMERICAN

3 eggs
⅛ tsp salt
pinch of pepper
butter
filling

Makes one omelette

For years we have enjoyed Peter's delicious omelettes, and here we have his step-by-step method. Make each person's omelette individually; as each one can be made in less than thirty seconds, several can be done very quickly. They are best when served immediately, but if necessary can be kept warm for a few minutes in a moderate oven.

1. A secret to making good omelettes is to use a thick iron pan, to use it only for making omelettes and to keep it clean. If it is dirty, never wash it; rather heat it, fill it with salt, heat the salt for a minute or two, then empty the pan and wipe it out well with a dry cloth.
2. Beat eggs with salt and pepper in a bowl. Do not add water or milk.
3. Heat the pan over a very hot flame. When it is smoking, add a piece of butter about the size of a walnut.
4. Let butter melt, and just before the butter turns brown—
5. Pour in the eggs.

6. Shake pan forward and backwards with one hand, and with the other hand stir eggs with a fork.
7. Add a spoonful or two of filling. (Fillings next page.)
8. Tip the pan and roll omelette down.
9. Let omelette sit for a moment, to firm.
10. Holding the plate at an angle—
11. Tip omelette out onto a plate.
12. Shape omelette with hands.

Fillings

The following recipes each make enough
for four omelettes.

Mushroom Filling

METRIC/IMPERIAL

455g/1 lb fresh
mushrooms

4oz butter

⅛ tsp salt

1. Wipe mushrooms clean, then slice.
2. Fry in butter until just tender. Add salt.

AMERICAN

8 cups fresh sliced
mushrooms

8 Tbsp butter

⅛ tsp salt

Tomato Cheese Filling

METRIC/IMPERIAL

225g/8oz fresh
tomatoes

110g/4oz cheese

1. Peel and chop tomatoes.
2. Grate cheese.
3. Fill omelette with tomatoes, then sprinkle tomatoes with
   grated cheese.

AMERICAN

1 cup fresh chopped
tomatoes

1 cup grated cheese

Peter's Favourite: Aubergine Filling

METRIC/IMPERIAL

1 clove garlic

60g/2oz onion

110g/4oz aubergine

60g/2oz fresh
tomato

60g/2oz fresh
mushrooms

60g/2oz green
pepper

60g/2oz butter

¼ tsp salt

1. Peel garlic. Peel and finely chop onion, aubergine and
   tomato. Wipe mushrooms clean, then chop. Wash and
   chop green pepper.
2. Melt butter in a frying pan. Put garlic through a garlic
   press; squeeze into frying pan. Add remaining vegetables
   and salt; slowly fry until completely tender, and almost
   sauce-like.

AMERICAN

1 clove garlic

½ cup onion

1 cup eggplant
(aubergine)

½ cup fresh tomato

1 cup fresh
mushrooms

½ cup green pepper

4 Tbsp butter

¼ tsp salt

Dutch Kale

Serve with sliced tomatoes topped with yogurt.

METRIC/IMPERIAL

225g/8oz butter, unsalted if possible

1 tsp tarragon

½ tsp thyme

2kg/4lbs potatoes

1kg/2lbs kale

340g/12oz cheese, preferably Edam

¼ litre/½ pint milk

pinch of pepper

2 egg yolks

2 egg whites

Makes 8 servings

AMERICAN

1 cup butter, unsalted if possible

1 tsp tarragon

½ tsp thyme

12 medium boiling potatoes

2 lbs kale

3 cups grated cheese, preferably Edam

1 cup milk

pinch of pepper

2 egg yolks

2 egg whites

Makes 8 servings

1. Melt butter slowly. Add tarragon and thyme. Simmer sauce very slowly until serving time. The long cooking time is necessary to achieve its nut-like flavour.
2. Wash potatoes; steam until tender.
3. Wash kale and remove leaves from stem, then steam until tender. Allow kale to cool, then chop very fine. If you wish, add some of the kale cooking water to the butter sauce.
4. Grate cheese.
5. Mash potatoes, allowing steam to evaporate, then thoroughly mix in kale, cheese, milk, pepper and egg yolks.
6. Beat egg whites until stiff, and fold into potato mixture.
7. Spoon into greased baking dish.
8. Bake at 190°C/Gas Mark 5/375°F for 30 minutes, or until hot and slightly browned on top.
9. To serve, spoon a portion onto a plate, make a little well in the potatoes and ladle sauce into the well.

Spinach Beans

METRIC/IMPERIAL

170g/6oz white kidney beans or any white bean

½ tsp sage

680ml/24fl oz water

2 onions

3 stalks celery

4 cloves garlic

3 Tbsp olive oil

½ tsp salt

pinch of pepper

2 Tbsp chopped parsley

½ tsp basil

455g/1 lb spinach

30g/1oz parmesan cheese, grated

Makes 6 servings

AMERICAN

1 cup white kidney beans or any white bean

½ tsp sage

3 cups water

2 onions

3 stalks celery

4 cloves garlic

¼ cup olive oil

½ tsp salt

pinch of pepper

2 Tbsp chopped parsley

½ tsp basil

1 lb spinach

¼ cup grated parmesan cheese

Makes 6 servings

1. Wash and sort beans. Combine with sage and water and bring to a boil, then remove from heat until all beans have sunk to the bottom. Once again bring to a boil, then simmer until tender (about 1½ hours). Drain beans, saving the cooking water.
2. Chop onions and celery; finely chop garlic.
3. In a large saucepan heat olive oil, then sauté garlic for a minute. Add onions and celery; continue to sauté until tender.
4. Add cooking water, salt, pepper, parsley, basil to onion mixture; cook for 10 minutes.
5. Stir in the beans, then lay spinach over the top.
6. Put top on the saucepan and steam until spinach is done. It may be necessary to add water.
7. Stir spinach into bean mixture, then spoon into serving dish.
8. Sprinkle parmesan cheese over all, and serve.

Peasant Pie

Pastry

115g/4oz flour

½ tsp salt

2½ Tbsp sesame seeds

55g/2oz shortening

140ml/3 Tbsp butter-milk or soured milk

Filling

5fl oz soured cream

¼ tsp dill

4 eggs

455g/1 lb cabbage

170g/6oz leeks or onions

30g/1oz butter

1 Tbsp lemon juice

225g/8oz mushrooms

¼ tsp basil

¼ tsp tarragon

¼ tsp marjoram

salt to taste

Makes 6 servings

AMERICAN

Pastry

1 cup flour

½ tsp salt

3 Tbsp sesame seeds

⅓ cup shortening

3 Tbsp buttermilk or soured milk

Filling

¾ cup sour cream

¼ tsp dill

4 eggs

1 small head cabbage

2 leeks or onions

2 Tbsp butter

1 Tbsp lemon juice

½ lb mushrooms

¼ tsp basil

¼ tsp tarragon

¼ tsp marjoram

salt to taste

Makes 6 servings

Instructions for Pastry

1. Mix together flour, salt and sesame seeds.
2. Cut in shortening until dough resembles small peas.
3. Add enough buttermilk to bring pastry together in a ball. This part can be done in advance, and, in fact, the pastry is easier to work and is flakier if it has been chilled for a while. Remove from refrigerator 30 minutes before using, if it has been chilled for a long time.

Instructions for Filling

1. Mix soured cream and dill together. Set aside.
2. Hard-cook the eggs. Peel and slice.
3. Clean the cabbage, cut in quarters, remove the hard core, then chop cabbage into bite-sized pieces. Steam until barely tender. Drain well.
4. Prepare leeks by making a lengthwise slit with a knife, and thoroughly washing out any dirt that might be trapped inside. Remove wilted parts. Chop leeks into bite-sized segments, and sauté in butter and lemon juice until tender. Drain.
5. Slice mushrooms and leave them raw.
6. Mix together cabbage, leeks, mushrooms, basil, tarragon and marjoram. Taste the mixture and add salt if needed.

Assembly

1. Preheat oven to 205°C/Gas Mark 6/400°F.
2. Roll out ⅔ of the pastry dough and fit into bottom and sides of a medium-sized baking dish.
3. Spread soured cream-dill mixture over bottom of pie, followed by sliced eggs, then vegetable mixture.
4. Roll out remaining ⅓ of pastry dough and place on top of pie, joining it to bottom crust by pinching edges together.
5. Make decorative slashes in top of pie, so that steam can escape.
6. Bake for 15 minutes, then lower heat to 180°C/ Gas Mark 4/350°F, and continue baking for 20 minutes more, or until light brown.

Variations

The basic ingredients of a peasant pie are vegetables, a sauce and a pastry crust.
The variations are endless.
Once you have become familiar with preparing the pie, try using different vegetables.
Or for another change of flavour, in place of the soured cream substitute a white sauce
or any other sauce or gravy. (This is a good way to use left-overs.)

Chickpea Casserole

This is a delicious way to use dry bread.

METRIC/IMPERIAL

140g/5oz chickpeas

680ml/24fl oz water

½ tsp sage

170g/6oz dry bread

110g/4oz onion, chopped

110g/4oz celery and leaves, chopped

2 Tbsp oil

15g/½oz parsley, chopped

1 egg

¼ tsp cayenne

1 tsp salt

1 Tbsp tamari

110g/4oz cheese, grated

Makes 4-6 servings

AMERICAN

1 cup chickpeas (garbanzo beans)

3 cups water

½ tsp sage

2 cups dry bread

1 cup chopped onion

1 cup chopped celery and leaves

2 Tbsp oil

¼ cup chopped parsley

1 egg

¼ tsp cayenne

1 tsp salt

1 Tbsp tamari

1 cup grated cheese

Makes 4-6 servings

1. Wash and sort chickpeas. Combine with water and sage in a saucepan. To reduce cooking time, soak beans overnight; otherwise, bring beans to a boil, then turn heat off and leave until chickpeas sink to the bottom. (About 15 minutes.) Bring to a boil again and simmer until completely tender. (About 2 hours.)
2. If possible, cut dry bread into cubes. Pour cooking water from beans over the bread and let bread completely soak up the water. Even the hardest pieces should soften. If there isn't enough water left from cooking the beans, add a little.
3. Preheat oven to 180°C/Gas Mark 4/350°F.
4. Sauté onions and celery in oil.
5. In a large mixing bowl mash chickpeas thoroughly, then add soaked bread and mash the two together. This can be done in an electric mixer or with a potato masher.
6. Add onions, celery, parsley, egg, cayenne, salt and tamari, and mix thoroughly. Taste for saltiness and add more tamari if needed.
7. Spoon into a greased baking dish and top with grated cheese.
8. Bake for 40 minutes or until golden brown.

Indonesian Meal by Erik

Nasi goreng (fried rice), marinated tofu with peanut sauce, garlic bananas, sambal oelek (hot sauce), salad and garnishes.
Fresh papaya, with a slice of lemon, is suggested for dessert.

Sambal Oelek

If you live near Indonesian food stores, you can purchase this sauce. This recipe is for a large amount; stored in a clean container in the freezer the sauce will keep almost indefinitely.

All the elements of this meal will make 8 servings, except for the sauce, where the recipe is for a large amount

METRIC/IMPERIAL

12 tomatoes or 18 tinned tomatoes, drained

2 small lemons

20 rawit peppers (very hot, small red peppers)

1 litre/1½ pints water

15 shallots

4 bulbs garlic

2 tsp sugar

2 tsp salt

¼ litre/½ pint sweet Chinese soya sauce

All the elements of this meal will make 8 servings, except for the sauce, where the recipe is for a large amount.

AMERICAN

12 tomatoes or 18 canned tomatoes, drained

2 small lemons

20 rawit peppers (very hot, small red peppers)

4 cups water

15 shallots

4 bulbs garlic

2 tsp sugar

2 tsp salt

1 cup sweet Chinese soya sauce

1. Peel tomatoes and chop fine.
2. Grate rind from one lemon; juice both lemons.
3. Wearing rubber gloves, chop peppers very fine. Wash gloves and hands immediately afterwards, and be careful not to touch face with hands, as peppers are very strong.
4. Put peppers in saucepan with water. Bring to a boil, then add tomatoes and simmer for 10 minutes.
5. Chop shallots very fine. Break garlic bulbs into cloves; peel cloves, then squeeze through a press and chop what remains in the press.
6. Fry shallots in small amount of oil. When transparent add garlic and fry until golden.
7. Add shallots and garlic to peppers, as well as sugar, salt, soya sauce, lemon juice and rind.
8. Bring to a boil and stir while boiling for 15 minutes.
9. Reduce heat, cover and simmer for 4-5 hours. Be careful not to burn sauce. Put an asbestos pad or a heat spreader between saucepan and heat. If sauce gets too thick, add water. If not thick enough, boil for a few minutes. When finished, sauce should be consistency of jam or marmalade. Store in a clean container with a tight lid.

Salad

This can be made a day in advance.

1. Wash and chop all vegetables into very small cubes.
2. Combine with yogurt, lemon juice, and salt and pepper to taste.
3. Place in a covered container in a cool place for at least four hours.

METRIC/IMPERIAL	AMERICAN
1 carrot	1 carrot
110g/4oz cauliflower	¼ of a medium-sized cauliflower
½ cucumber	½ cucumber
1 red bell pepper	1 red bell pepper
2 Tbsp chopped fresh parsley	2 Tbsp chopped fresh parsley
chives	chives
2 gherkin pickles	2 gherkin pickles
¼ litre/½ pint yogurt	1 cup yogurt
juice of ½ lemon	juice of ½ lemon
salt and pepper	salt and pepper

Tofu

1. Cut tofu into chunks and arrange in one layer in a glass baking dish.
2. Put remaining ingredients in a blender and process until smooth. Pour over tofu and marinate for 2-3 hours.
3. Bake tofu at 210°C/Gas Mark 6/400°F for 30 minutes, or until piping hot.
4. Serve tofu with peanut sauce spooned over.
5. Strain leftover marinade, and use for another meal.

METRIC/IMPERIAL	AMERICAN
680g/24oz tofu	4½ cups tofu
¼ litre/½ pint tamari	1 cup tamari
¼ litre/½ pint water	1 cup water
3 cloves garlic	3 cloves garlic
15g/½oz ginger root	3 tsp grated ginger root

Peanut Sauce

METRIC/IMPERIAL

1 tsp lemon rind

1 Tbsp lemon juice

1 tsp orange rind

1 onion

5 cloves garlic

1 tsp grated ginger root

oil

225g/8oz smooth peanut butter

boiling water

1 tsp sambal oelek (hot sauce)

2 Tbsp sweet Chinese soya sauce

2 tsp brown sugar

½ tsp salt

AMERICAN

1 tsp lemon rind

1 Tbsp lemon juice

1 tsp orange rind

1 onion

5 cloves garlic

1 tsp grated ginger root

oil

1 cup smooth peanut butter

boiling water

1 tsp sambal oelek (hot sauce)

2 Tbsp sweet Chinese soya sauce

2 tsp brown sugar

½ tsp salt

1. Grate rind of lemon, then juice it. Grate orange rind.
2. Finely chop onion and garlic; grate ginger root.
3. Sauté onion in oil. When tender, add garlic and ginger; fry lightly.
4. Thin peanut butter with hot boiling water until it is the thickness of running honey.
5. Gently heat peanut butter in a heavy saucepan or in the top of a double saucepan over boiling water.
6. Add onions, garlic, ginger, lemon juice and rind, orange rind, sambal oelek, soya sauce and sugar.
7. Mix thoroughly; then taste to see if salt is needed before adding it.
8. Simmer for ½ hour. Do not allow to boil. Add more water if sauce gets too thick.

Emergency

If by some mistake sauce separates because it has been allowed to boil, mix a little arrowroot with cold water and add to sauce.

Garnishes

METRIC/IMPERIAL

280g/10oz peanuts

90g/3oz coconut

AMERICAN

2 cups peanuts

1 cup coconut

1. Preheat oven to 180°C/Gas Mark 4/350°F.
2. In separate pans, roast peanuts and coconut, turning often. When roasted, mix together.
3. Serve on the table in bowls, or sprinkle over food on served plate.

Garlic Bananas

8 very ripe bananas

juice of ½ lemon

3 Tbsp garlic powder

8 very ripe bananas

juice of ½ lemon

3 Tbsp garlic powder

1. Peel and slice bananas.
2. Place bananas, lemon juice and garlic powder in electric mixer bowl and whip at a slow speed for ½ hour. This process is what gives the dish its characteristic fluffiness.
3. Put bananas into greased flat baking dish.
4. Bake at 170°C/Gas Mark 3/335°F for 20 minutes.

Nasi Goreng

¾ litre/1½ pints water

340g/12oz brown rice

¼ tsp salt

1 large onion

3 cloves garlic

3 tsp grated ginger root

1 large carrot

3 red bell peppers

45g/1½oz parsley, chopped fine

170g/6oz peas

170g/6oz bamboo shoots

1 firm tomato

oil

3 tsp sambal oelek (or more)

2 tsp sugar

pinch of turmeric

3 cups water

1½ cups brown rice

¼ tsp salt

1 large onion

3 cloves garlic

3 tsp grated ginger root

1 large carrot

3 red bell peppers

¾ cup finely chopped parsley

1 cup peas

¾ cup bamboo shoots

1 firm tomato

oil

3 tsp sambal oelek (or more)

2 tsp sugar

pinch of turmeric

1. Bring water to a boil. Wash rice and drain.
2. Add rice and salt to boiling water. Bring to a boil again, then reduce heat and simmer, covered, for 40 minutes, or until rice is just tender. *Do not overcook.*
3. Wash and chop vegetables. Leave peas whole. Peel tomatoes before chopping. Garlic should be minced and vegetables should be thinly sliced to cook quickly. Experiment with different kinds of cutting, to accentuate the beauty of the vegetables.
4. In a wok or frying pan, fry onions in oil. When tender, add garlic and ginger, then remaining vegetables and seasonings. Add a few drops of water; cover wok.
5. When vegetables are tender, stir in hot rice.
6. Rice can be kept warm in a covered dish in a moderate oven, or served immediately.

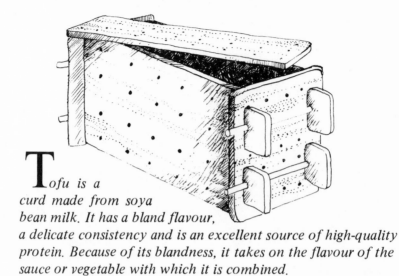

Tofu is a curd made from soya bean milk. It has a bland flavour, a delicate consistency and is an excellent source of high-quality protein. Because of its blandness, it takes on the flavour of the sauce or vegetable with which it is combined.

Fresh tofu is best; if you do not live near a shop which supplies fresh tofu, you can quite easily make it yourself at home. In the next few pages, we will present the method we use, which was developed by Jacques Cormier, pictured here. The equipment being used is quite large, as the tofu is being made for a large number of people. You can, however, use the same method with normal kitchen equipment.

If you become intrigued with the art of making tofu, and would like to have more tofu recipes, as well as information about this centuries-old tradition, we highly recommend reading The Book of Tofu by William Shurtleff and Akiko Aoyagi (Autumn Press, 1975).

Homemade Tofu

The recipe given here yields approximately 1kg/2 lbs tofu. Make a smaller amount if you don't think you can use it all within two or three days.

455g/1 lb soya beans

Solidifier
(choose one):

*1½ Tbsp nigari**

1 Tbsp Epsom salts

6 Tbsp lemon juice

570ml/1 pint freshly collected seawater

*nigari is usually available at natural food stores

AMERICAN

2½ cups soy beans

Solidifier
(choose one):

*1½ Tbsp nigari**

1 Tbsp Epsom salts

6 Tbsp lemon juice

2½ cups freshly collected seawater

*nigari is usually available at natural food stores

Special Equipment

blender

cooking thermometer

colander

cheesecloth or thin cotton dish towel

settling container: either use colander *or* a wooden box with removable lid and perforations on all sides; it should be able to be completely disassembled for ease in cleaning

large soup pot

Special Equipment

blender

cooking thermometer

colander

cheesecloth or thin cotton dish towel

settling container: either use colander *or* a wooden box with removable lid and perforations on all sides; it should be able to be completely disassembled for ease in cleaning

large soup pot

1. Wash and sort soya beans, then soak in about four times as much cold water for 8-12 hours. In case of emergency, if you need to speed soaking time, use hot water.
2. The beans are ready when they are white inside.
3. Drain beans and rinse well under cold running water.
4. Measure the total amount of beans in a measuring jug, then put twice that amount of water into a large soup pot to heat.

5. Put an equal amount of beans and hot water into a blender. (Incidentally, this is not the same hot water that is heating on stove.) Fill blender at least half full, to insure that beans blend well, but not more than ¾ full, as it might overflow. If blender does overflow, clean up the mess immediately, as it gets very sticky if left too long. Don't be discouraged if you make a mess the first time through; next time you will be more familiar with the capacity of your equipment. Depending upon the amount of beans and the size of the blender, you may need to do several batches. Process beans for about 3 minutes, or until very smooth.

6. Add blended soya bean purée to water heating in the soup pot.
7. Heat mixture to 77°C(170°F).
8. Line a colander with a double thickness of cheesecloth, or a thin cotton towel. Place the colander over a deep bowl. Ladle hot soya bean purée into cheesecloth.
9. Wearing insulated rubber gloves to protect hands from heat, gather up the cheesecloth and squeeze out as much milk as possible, tourniquet-style. If you don't wish to use rubber gloves, twist the cheesecloth, then press with the end of a glass jar or mug.

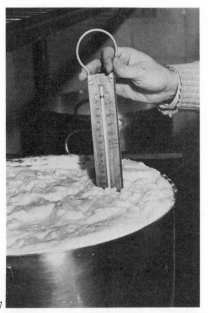
7

8

9

71

10. Save the remaining pulp and use it as a nutritious extender in casseroles, cat food, chicken food or bread.
11. If making a large amount of tofu, use two colanders simultaneously. While one is draining, the other can be squeezed.
12. As soon as pan is empty, wash it immediately, as it gets incredibly sticky otherwise. This applies to all utensils used.
Note: If you wish to make soya milk, the process is complete at this point.
13. Pour soya milk back into pot, and heat again.

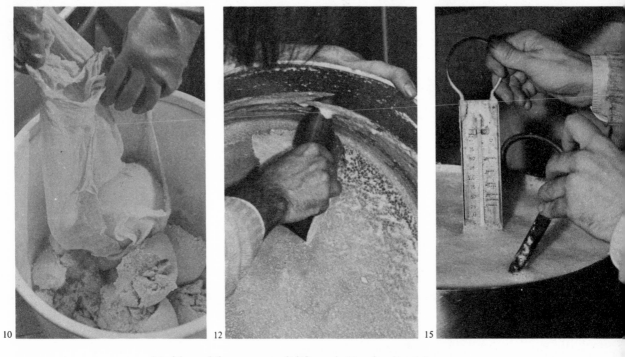

14. Meanwhile, prepare solidifier solution, by dissolving solidifier in 570ml/1 pint/2½ cups water. (If using seawater, it is not necessary to add more water.) Note: if using soured soya milk, solidifier is usually not necessary.
15. Bring soya milk to 93°C(200°F).
16. Remove pan from heat. Gently stir soya milk around in pot; then while stirring add one-third of the solidifier solution. Bring stirring to a halt, hold spoon upright for a moment until all movement ceases, then remove. Sprinkle another third of solidifier solution over the top of soya milk.
17. Leave pot for 3 or 4 minutes, without stirring, and watch curds start to form.

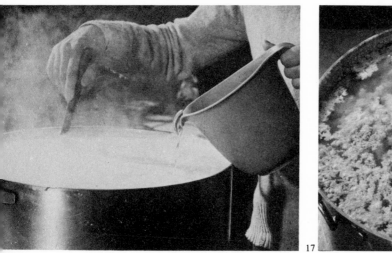

17

18. Gently cut into pot with wooden spoon, to see if curds have formed throughout. If necessary, add final third of solidifier, gently stirring into just the top of the pot. Leave for another 3 minutes. If curds still haven't formed sufficiently, add more solidifier.
19. Mixture should definitely have separated into white curds of tofu, floating in a clear whey. There should not be any milky liquid remaining.
20. To remove whey, press a strainer into the pot and ladle out the whey. Save whey to be used in making soup or bread. Or flavour with tamari and drink as a broth.
21. Place the settling container or colander over a large pan to catch the whey. Line the container with cheesecloth, then moisten cheesecloth with whey. Ladle curds into container very gently, so as not to break them.

19

20   21

22   23

22. Fold ends of cheesecloth over, and put top in place (or put a plate on top, if using a colander).
23. Press moisture out.
24. Place a weight on top until whey no longer drips from holes. *Or* leave tofu in box for 6-8 hours and let its own weight press whey out.
25. Fill a sink with water and immerse settling container in it, upside down.
26. Remove settling container. Notice that top is still under the tofu.
27. Gently turn tofu on its side and remove top.
28. Unwrap cheesecloth.
29. Carefully lift tofu from water.
30. Store it, refrigerated, in water in a covered container. Change water daily if tofu is not used immediately.

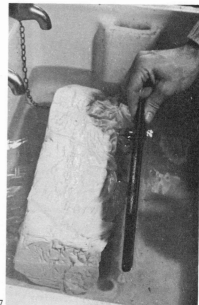

26

27

29

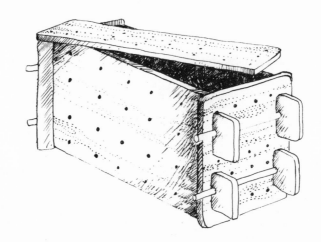

Salads

*When you make a salad, as you handle each vegetable or herb,
let your mind dwell on how each was made. You can feel
the struggle that some of them have had to pull through,
whereas with others you can feel the ease and freedom in which
they have been brought to fruition. All these thoughts and feelings
are important. They bring the very life force into your body.*

Eileen's guidance

I f you have a garden, a lovely daily ritual is the gathering of fresh vegetables and herbs for salads. Whereas salads are delicious when simple—lettuce with olive oil, lemon juice and a few fresh herbs—they have now also expanded to include nearly every vegetable and often to take a more important role as the central part of a meal.

In choosing vegetables for a salad, pick the most vital-looking ones with plenty of obvious energy. And use them as quickly as possible after harvesting, to maintain that energy.

Salads are enhanced by tasty dressings, and made more filling by the addition of various garnishes. Sprouted beans and grains add variety and nourishment to the salad, and have the advantage of being available year-round. In the next few pages all of these aspects of salad making will be presented. Whether or not you grow them yourself, eating fresh raw vegetables strengthens and purifies you for the tasks ahead.

Preparing Salad

Many vegetables which wouldn't ordinarily be considered for salads make perfect salad additions when grated. Root vegetables, such as beetroot (beets), turnips and Jerusalem artichokes, are particularly good. They should be grated just before serving.

Make a salad vegetable of tough winter greens by cutting them very thin with scissors.

Edible wild plants and flowers can be added to the salad for variety.

To make salad preparation easier, wash salad greens when you have a few minutes, then wrap them, with the moisture still on the leaves, in a towel. Keep in the refrigerator until needed.

Dressings

Mayonnaise

AMERICAN

4 eggs, room
temperature

1 tsp dry mustard

1 tsp salt

¼ tsp cayenne

2 Tbsp vinegar

oil

METRIC/IMPERIAL

4 eggs, room
temperature

1 tsp dry mustard

1 tsp salt

¼ tsp cayenne

2 Tbsp vinegar

oil

1. Put all ingredients into a blender jar, using 2 Tbsp oil to begin.
2. Process at low speed; with blender running, remove the small inner part of the lid and very slowly drizzle in oil. Keep adding oil, and as mayonnaise begins to thicken, remove lid and watch it. As it whirls around there will be a hole in the centre. The second that the hole closes, stop adding oil immediately. If the mayonnaise is to be used as salad dressing, it is finished at this point.
   Emergency: If the whole thing falls apart, as it sometimes does, pour the dressing out of the blender, break another egg into the blender, then slowly add the fallen-apart dressing to the egg, with the blender running. Only add it until the hole closes, then STOP. (You probably added too much oil the first time, and that's why it fell apart.)
3. If you would like an even thicker mayonnaise, remove from blender and whisk in more oil by hand, adding it very slowly.

Variation

We used to have a lot of friendly competition to see who could come up with the most outrageously flavoured mayonnaise. Bobananda won the competition and goes down in history for his carob mayonnaise (add carob powder to taste to above recipe). For some rather more conventional flavours, blend with the basic recipe spring onions, garlic, parsley, cucumber, tomatoes or your favourite herb.

Tomato Yogurt Dressing

3 tomatoes

½ litre/1 pint yogurt

3 large sprigs of parsley

1½ tsp basil

1½ tsp oregano

1½ tsp garlic powder

1½ tsp celery powder

1 tsp salt (optional)

*Makes ¾ litre/
1¼ pints/¾ quart*

1. Purée all ingredients in a blender. The dressing should be thick and creamy.
2. If you wish a thinner dressing, add milk.

AMERICAN

3 tomatoes

2 cups yogurt

3 large sprigs of parsley

1½ tsp basil

1½ tsp oregano

1½ tsp garlic powder

1½ tsp celery powder

1 tsp salt (optional)

Makes ¾ quart

Chartres Cathedral Dressing

METRIC/IMPERIAL

¼ litre/½ pint lemon juice

¼ litre/½ pint orange juice

½ litre/1 pint oil

3 tsp mustard powder

1½ tsp garlic powder

½ tsp parsley

¼ tsp paprika

2 tsp marjoram

¼ tsp salt

4 tsp sugar

pinch of pepper

pinch of cayenne

*Makes 1 litre/
2 pints/1 quart*

When Paul makes this salad dressing, it takes him three hours, observers say, and he uses the same care and concentration that went into the building of Chartres Cathedral. One thing he regularly does is make a mistake and add too much of something, so much of the three hours is spent in correcting the mistake but the salad dressing comes out even better in these cases for some reason. So make some mistakes and take three hours and you've got the dressing. Or you can just whip it together in a few minutes. It's still good.

1. Pour lemon juice and orange juice through a strainer into a jar.
2. Add remaining ingredients and shake the jar.

Serving Suggestion: This goes well over a salad of lettuce and avocado; or a spinach salad with tomato, cucumber and bits of hard-cooked egg, chopped fine.

AMERICAN

1 cup lemon juice

1 cup orange juice

2½ cups oil

3 tsp mustard powder

1½ tsp garlic powder

½ tsp parsley

¼ tsp paprika

2 tsp marjoram

¼ tsp salt

4 tsp sugar

pinch of pepper

pinch of cayenne

Makes 1 quart

Tahini Dressing

The simplest dressing, yet one of the best

METRIC/IMPERIAL

¼ litre/½ pint tahini

¼ litre/½ pint cold water

about 2-3 Tbsp tamari

Makes ½ litre/1 pint/ 2 cups

1. Add water to tahini and whisk until water is completely absorbed and tahini has become fluffy.
2. Add tamari to taste.
3. For a thinner dressing, add more water.

AMERICAN

1 cup tahini

1 cup cold water

about 2-3 Tbsp tamari

Makes 2 cups

Honey Tamari Dressing

METRIC/IMPERIAL

2 Tbsp finely chopped spring onion

455ml/16fl oz safflower oil

110ml/4fl oz lemon juice

225ml/8fl oz tamari

3 Tbsp honey

¼ tsp cayenne

2½ Tbsp sesame seeds

Makes 1 litre/2 pints/ 1 quart

1. Chop onions.
2. With a whisk, blend oil, lemon juice, tamari, honey and cayenne.
3. Add onions and sesame seeds. Whisk a bit more.
4. Before serving, whisk the dressing again.

AMERICAN

2 Tbsp finely chopped green onion

2 cups safflower oil

½ cup lemon juice

1 cup tamari

4 Tbsp honey

½ tsp cayenne

3 Tbsp sesame seeds

Makes 1 quart

Essence of Sprouts Dressing

METRIC/IMPERIAL

4 cloves garlic

340 ml/12fl oz olive oil

110ml/4fl oz lemon juice

3 Tbsp tamari

110g/4oz alfalfa or bean sprouts

Makes ½ litre/1 pint/ 2 cups

1. Peel garlic.
2. Process all ingredients in blender until smooth.
3. Refrigerate dressing and use within two days.

Variation

For a different taste, instead of adding sprouts, add parsley, chives, cucumber or tomato.

AMERICAN

4 cloves garlic

1½ cups olive oil

½ cup lemon juice

3 Tbsp tamari

2 cups alfalfa or bean sprouts

Makes 2 cups

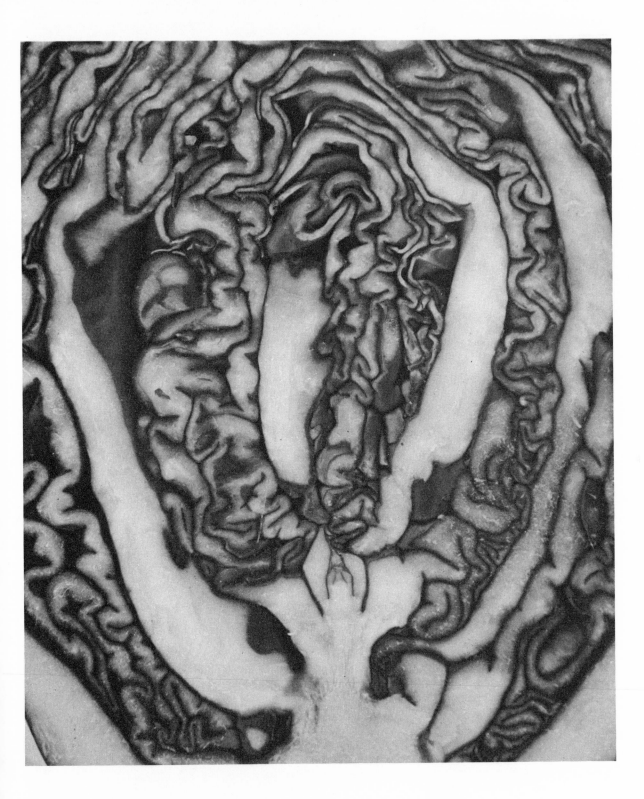

Garnishes

These little additions can give a plain salad real pizazz.
They're also great with soup.

Garlic Croûtons

METRIC/IMPERIAL

170g/6oz bread
4 cloves garlic
60g/2oz butter

AMERICAN

4 slices bread
4 cloves garlic
4 Tbsp butter

1. Cut bread into cubes, then spread out on an ungreased baking tin.
2. Bake at the lowest heat in your oven for 1-2 hours, or until bread is dry and hard. Or if you are in a hurry, bake at 180°C/Gas Mark 4/350°F for about ½ hour, stirring frequently.
3. For plain croûtons, the process is finished at this point. Store croûtons in an air-tight container.
4. Just before serving time, peel and chop garlic, then sauté in butter.
5. When garlic is golden, add croûtons and sauté until completely warmed and slightly browned.
6. Serve over salad. The combination of cold salad and hot, garlicky croûtons is quite nice.

Variation

For herb croûtons, sauté dry croûtons in butter with 1 tsp herbs added: such as basil, oregano, marjoram or thyme. Or sauté them in 4 Tbsp olive oil, ⅛ tsp salt and 1 tsp herbs.

Gomasio

METRIC/IMPERIAL

Seven parts sesame seeds

one part salt

AMERICAN

Seven parts sesame seeds

one part salt

The favourite condiment for everything.

1. Heat a heavy frying pan over a high flame.
2. When frying pan is hot, add seeds, lower heat and roast seeds, stirring occasionally, for just a few minutes, or until they are beginning to turn golden. Add salt and continue roasting until seeds are done (when they crush easily and taste completely roasted).
3. When seeds and salt have cooled, grind in a mortar and pestel or a nut grinder. They should be ground to a powder, with a few seeds left whole for flavour.
4. Store in an air-tight jar. Make in small amounts, so that it can be used within a week.

Tamari Nuts

Spread peanuts in one layer in a large baking tin. Place on the bottom rack of the oven and roast at 180°C/Gas Mark 4/350°F for 30-60 minutes, stirring occasionally. When nicely browned, remove from oven and immediately sprinkle tamari over nuts, while stirring with a wooden spoon. Add enough tamari that they taste salty, but not so much that there is tamari left in the pan. The tamari should all evaporate as they are stirred.

Variations
Use the same method for cashews, almonds, sunflower seeds, pumpkin seeds. Sprinkle with ground ginger, garlic powder or onion powder.

Seaweed

METRIC/IMPERIAL

30g/1oz sea-weed

1 onion

4 cloves garlic

2 tsp grated ginger

oil

1 Tbsp tamari

AMERICAN

2 cups sea-weed

1 onion

4 cloves garlic

2 tsp grated ginger

oil

1 Tbsp tamari

*Yes, you read it right: sea-weed.
It's delicious when prepared well, full of nutrients, and people tend to crave it after discovering they like it. And it's a great side garnish with a salad, or with rice. If you live near a source of fresh sea-weed, by all means use it. Other wise, you can obtain it in its dried form from whole food shops. Even the severest critics usually like sea-weed prepared this way.*

1. In a saucepan, cover sea-weed with water. Simmer, covered, until tender. The time varies greatly, depending on the type of sea-weed. It is done when tender, like lasagne noodles. Test it with your fingernail. If the smell of the sea-weed cooking is more than you can bear, start frying the onion, garlic and ginger, to cover the smell. (Confessions of a former sea-weed detester.)
2. Drain sea-weed and chop into bite-sized segments.
3. Peel and finely chop onion and garlic. Fry onion, garlic and ginger in oil until tender.
4. Add sea-weed and fry a half minute longer, then mix in tamari.

Mung beans, alfalfa seeds, chick peas, aduki beans, fenugreek seeds, radish seeds, lentils, wheat: almost any whole natural seed, bean or grain will sprout.

Sprouts

Watching something grow out of that tiny seed, seeing a small green bit pop out, is a never-ending miracle.

To grow sprouts, soak seeds overnight, then leave them in indirect light, rinsing twice daily until ready. *Please remember* that essential simplicity to the process. In the next few pages we have photographed and described every detail; this is because the sprouts inspired us, not because the process is complicated.

The pictures demonstrate our method of making sprouts for 150 people. We have used the equipment and space available to us. I'm certain there are more sophisticated systems, yet ours does manage to produce a lot of sprouts; and the initial cash outlay was minimal. Of course, if you are making sprouts at home, you will be growing only one or two jars at a time, but the process is still the same. And the rewards are many. Not only do salads become more filling, satisfying and nourishing, but handling sprouts is a daily reminder that the life force is at work.

1. Put seeds in a jar. (Seeds can be obtained at whole food shops. They must be live, and not chemically treated.) For alfalfa seeds, use 3 Tbsp for a 1 litre/2 pint/1 quart jar. (For all other seeds and beans, fill the jar ¼ full.) We use the jars that are available to us, but it would be better to use a wide mouth jar, for ease in draining water later.
2. Fill jar half full with cold water.
3. Leave seeds to soak overnight.
4. In the morning, put a piece of cheesecloth or lacy material on the jar. The mesh must be large enough to let the water out easily, but not so large that the seeds escape.

5. Fasten the cheesecloth on very securely with a rubber band, as the seeds will be rinsed many times, and it is very disheartening to have a whole jar of seeds empty into the sink because the top has come loose.
6. Pour off soaking water and drain.
7. Leave seeds in indirect light, preferably at 30° tilt, so that any excess water can run out. Put them where they are easily accessible and visible, so that you will remember to rinse them. Some people leave them in the dish drainer. Sprouts must have even temperature and light to grow well. In the summer protect them from too much heat and sun; in the winter give them more light and warmth. NOTE: If you want to grow Chinese style long mung bean sprouts, grow them in complete darkness.
8. To rinse sprouts, fill jar with water.
9. Gently shake seeds and water around.
10. Drain water.
11. Leave bottles upside down for a few minutes, to let all the water drain; then return them to their growing spot. Continue rinsing sprouts twice a day until they are ready to be eaten.

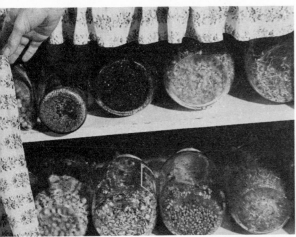

6

8

11

12. Sprouts are ready to be eaten when they have lost all their starchiness, and taste like a vegetable. This will take from one to ten days, depending on the type of sprout and the climate where you live. Try eating the sprouts at different lengths, to see what seems the most agreeable to you. Sunflower seed sprouts, however, should always be used before the sprouted part is as long as the seed. Alfalfa sprouts should be quite a bit longer than the others, and are ready when you can see two little leaves growing at the end of the sprout.

13. Note: The remainder of the process applies only to alfalfa sprouts. When sprouts have grown two leaves, put into a pan of cold water.

15

14. Gently break up any solid masses that may have developed.
15. Swish sprouts around in the water.
16. Scoop off hulls that float to the top.
17. When all hulls have been scooped off, pour water through a colander.
18. Some hulls also will have sunk to the bottom. Carefully pick sprouts from the hulls.
19. Now put the hulled sprouts into a larger jar, so that they have more room to grow. Or divide them between two jars.

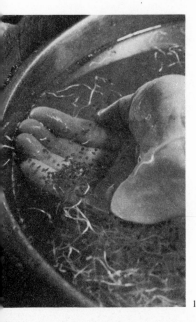

18

19

20. Put on a mesh cover.
21. Leave them upside down in a window where they will receive a lot of light, but not direct sunlight (although we do put them in direct sunlight here in Scotland, because the climate is cool). When they have turned green, they are ready to eat.

Breads

*Before, in the old, food provided the energy for building
or maintaining a solid physical body, but now, in the new,
it is the life force, the light which one absorbs that matters.*

Eileen's guidance

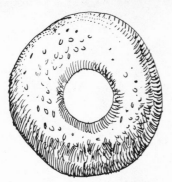

These recipes are some of the favourites from our bakery at Cluny Hill, which serves about 300 people each day. Early in the morning the bakers are already working, and by mid-morning the halls are full of the lovely smell of home-baked bread.

We use wholemeal flour in most of our bread. If you've never used it before, try growing accustomed to it slowly by first mixing it half and half with white. Wholemeal flour, like other whole grains, takes longer to bake than its refined counterpart. For bread baking, a strong, or hard, flour should be used. For pastries and cakes, use a soft flour.

If baking for a small family seems too much bother, note that most of these recipes are for large quantities: you put almost an equal amount of energy into the process, and half the bread can be frozen for later use.

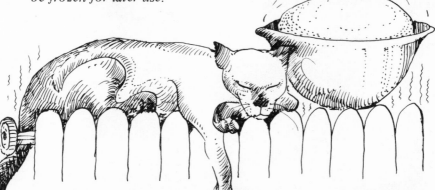

How do you know when the bread is done? For the beginner it can be a mystery. It should, of course, be golden brown on the outside. When removed from the baking tin, it should give a hollow sound when tapped on the bottom with a fist. Some can tell by the smell when the bread is done. If you're really in doubt, cut your first experimental loaves in half and inspect the inside. After two or three such inspections, you should begin to get a sense of what the bread looks like when it's done.

And finally, there's no denying the pleasure of baking bread: the smell in the house, the feeling of the dough under your hands, the delight in eating it and sharing it with family. It's another way to put love into the food you prepare.

Basic Wholemeal Bread

METRIC/IMPERIAL

1 Tbsp dry yeast

warm water

2 Tbsp honey

3.2kg/7 lbs wholemeal bread flour (or half wholemeal and half unbleached white)

2-3 Tbsp salt

about 2 litres/3 pints warm water

Makes 4 medium loaves

AMERICAN

1¼ Tbsp dry yeast

warm water

2 Tbsp honey

25 cups whole wheat bread flour (or half whole wheat and half unbleached white)

2-3 Tbsp salt

about 2 quarts warm water

Makes 4 medium loaves

1. Dissolve yeast in enough warm water to cover. Add honey; do not stir. Let sit until yeast 'mushrooms' (5 minutes or so).
2. Sift dry ingredients together.
3. When yeast looks frothy, stir well and add to flour mixture.
4. Add water until flour comes together into dough. Work with hands until the sides and bottom of the bowl are clean.
5. Work in oil; then knead for 5-10 minutes, until dough is supple, uniform in appearance, and 'fleshy' like an ear lobe or a baby's bottom.
6. Oil a bowl and place dough in it. Cover with a damp cloth and place in a warm spot in your kitchen or even a steamy bathroom. Let rise until double in size (about 1½ hours).
7. Oil bread pans now, or flat sheets for braids or rolls.
8. After bread doubles, punch it down well with your fist and let it sit for 10 or 15 minutes more.
9. Form dough into loaves and allow to rise for 30 minutes.
10. Bake at 210°C/Gas Mark 6/400°F for 45-55 minutes, or until done.

Shaping the Loaves

The time of shaping and decorating the bread can be your favourite time, and a moment for creativity and inspiration to flow. Here are some ideas to begin with.

Regular Loaf
Press dough into rectangle, fold in thirds. Press again in a rectangle, fold in thirds in the opposite direction. Press out again, then roll up and place in loaf pan, seam side down.

Round
Knead dough into round shape. Make slashes in top with sharp knife.

Diagonal Cuts
Make regular loaf, then make diagonal slashes in top of loaf with sharp knife or dough knife.

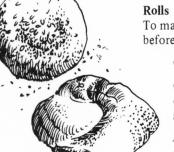

Rolls
To make rolls a uniform size, weigh each piece of dough before forming the roll.

Clover Leaf – 3 little balls of dough in oiled muffin tins.

Circular Twist – Make two strips of dough, and join at either end. Then twist in opposite directions, and curl around so that ends meet. Pinch together.

Round – Make balls of dough, then cut decorative slashes on top. Or sprinkle with poppy or sesame seeds.

Bake at 220°C/Gas Mark 7/425°F for about 20 minutes, or until browned.

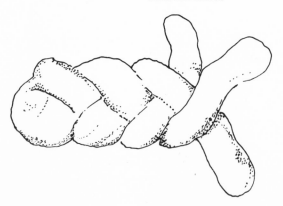

3 Plait (Braid)
Done just like plaiting hair.

Decorative additions
To any of these loaves or rolls, add a shiny crust by brushing with beaten egg to which 1 Tbsp water has been added. Sprinkle poppy seeds or sesame seeds over the top.

Variations for Wholemeal Bread

Cheese Bread
Roll out dough to a rectangular shape, and liberally spread grated cheese on it, leaving top and bottom edges with an empty margin. Start at top and roll dough into loaf. Place in pan as for a regular shaped loaf.

Cheese Plait
Work grated cheese into the dough (about 110g/4oz/1 cup for one loaf of bread), then cut into pieces for plaiting, as described previously. Cheese plaits are beautiful and very popular. Brush with egg wash and sprinkle with poppy or sesame seeds.

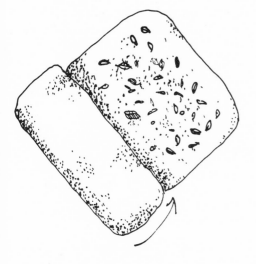

Herb Bread
Have about 3 or 4 favourite savoury herbs (1 tsp each) soaking in water. Some that do well are basil, thyme, rosemary, marjoram, sage or dill (the last two should be used sparingly as they are so strong). Roll out dough into a rectangle and spread with butter or margarine, then sprinkle drained soaked herbs on bread. Roll up bread and place in oiled pan. Brush with egg wash and sprinkle with seeds.

Cinnamon Raisin Bread
Have 85g/3oz/½ cup raisins soaking in hot water. Roll dough out in a rectangular shape, and spread with butter. Sprinkle drained raisins and 1 tsp cinnamon over all. Start at top and roll it tightly. Dab bottom edge with water to make dough stick together, and prick across the seam. Gently place, seam side down, in oiled loaf pan and brush with a glaze of 1 Tbsp melted butter, 1 Tbsp honey and ¼ tsp cinnamon. This loaf takes a little longer to bake than regular wheat bread. Check it after 50-60 minutes.

Sourdough Bread

Starter

450g/1 lb wholemeal
bread flour

warm water

Bread

1 Tbsp dry yeast

60g/2oz honey

450g/1 lb wholemeal
bread flour

¾ Tbsp salt

about 1 litre/2 pints
water

1 egg

Makes 1-2 loaves

AMERICAN

Starter

3½ cups whole wheat
bread flour

warm water

Bread

1¼ Tbsp dry yeast

3 Tbsp honey

3½ cups whole wheat
bread flour

1 Tbsp salt

about 1 quart water

1 egg

Makes 1-2 loaves

Starter

1. Mix flour and enough warm water to make a soupy mix.
   Let stand in covered container in refrigerator for as long
   as you like, from overnight to months. The longer it sits,
   the riper and more sour (and perhaps more tasty) the bread.

Bread

1. Dissolve yeast in enough warm water to cover it. Add
   honey. Let sit for a few minutes, or until the yeast
   mushrooms on its own, without stirring.
2. Mix flour and salt together.
3. Stir yeast mixture thoroughly and add to flour and salt.
4. Add this fairly dry mix to the starter (which is fairly wet)
   then slowly add flour or water until dough is of a
   consistency to be kneaded easily. Knead dough for about
   10 minutes, or until consistent and spongey.
5. Place in oiled bowl and cover with damp cloth. In a warm
   place, let rise until double in size (about 1½ hours).
6. Punch it down thoroughly, and let rise again, about
   ½ hour.
7. On a floured board, form into French style loaves by
   rolling a piece of dough with open hands until long and
   evenly shaped.
8. Place on oiled baking sheet, brush with egg wash (egg and
   a little water mixed well) and make diagonal slits in top
   of bread with sharp knife.
9. Bake at 170°C/Gas Mark 3/325°F for 45-50 minutes, or
   until light golden brown and hollow sounding on bottom
   when tapped.

Unleavened Flowers-Seed Bread

Unleavened breads fit nicely into a busy schedule, as they are left for 8-12 hours, or overnight, and finished later.

METRIC/IMPERIAL

1kg/2 lbs 6 oz wholemeal bread flour

1 Tbsp salt

2 Tbsp sesame seeds

6 Tbsp poppy seeds

5 Tbsp sunflower seeds

about ¾ litre/1½ pints water

poppy seeds

Makes 1-2 loaves

AMERICAN

8½ cups whole wheat bread flour

1 Tbsp salt

2½ Tbsp sesame seeds

½ cup poppy seeds

⅓ cup sunflower seeds

about 3 cups water

poppy seeds

Makes 1-2 loaves

1. Mix together dry ingredients and seeds.
2. Add water slowly, adding just enough to make dough come together to be kneaded. Watch the consistency as you mix it. It won't be fluffy and spongey like yeasted bread, but heavier and somewhat soft. Mix well.
3. Knead for 5 to 10 minutes, on a floured surface.
4. Place dough in oiled bowl, cover with damp towel; leave in a warm place for 8-12 hours, or overnight.
5. In the morning, knead for 5 minutes or so, working in the crusty top part of the dough.
6. Shape into loaves, then dip into poppy seeds. Place in an oiled loaf pan.
7. Bake at 170°C/Gas Mark 3/325°F for 1-1½ hours, or until crust on top is golden brown.
8. Cut bread very thin to serve.

Unleavened Old World Rye

Cut thin; serve with Swiss cheese and mustard.

METRIC/IMPERIAL

680g/1½ lbs wholemeal bread flour

680g/1½ lbs rye flour

1 Tbsp salt

1 Tbsp caraway seeds

85g/3oz sesame seeds

about 1 litre/2 pints water

Makes 1-2 loaves

AMERICAN

5¼ cups whole wheat bread flour

9 cups rye flour

1 Tbsp salt

1¼ Tbsp caraway seeds

½ cup sesame seeds

about 1 quart water

Makes 1-2 loaves

1. Mix dry ingredients and seeds together.
2. Slowly mix in water, adding just enough to bring dough together in a ball. Rye flour is much different to work with than wheat. The final consistency will be somewhat stickier than seed bread.
3. Knead for 5-10 minutes.
4. Place dough in oiled bowl, cover with a damp towel, and leave in a warm place for 8-12 hours, or overnight.
5. Knead for 5 minutes, then shape into long oval loaves.
6. Place on flat oiled baking tin and bake at 170°C/Gas Mark 3/325°F for 1-1½ hours or until golden and hollow sounding.

Soda Bread

*A bread which can be made in surprisingly little time;
the taste of soda bread brings memories
of the warm people and inviting hearths of Ireland.*

455g/1 lb bread flour

¾ tsp bicarbonate of soda

¾ tsp salt

¾ tsp sugar or honey

¼ litre/½ pint sour milk or buttermilk

1 egg

Makes 1 loaf

3½ cups bread flour

1 tsp baking soda

1 tsp salt

1 tsp sugar or honey

1 cup sour milk or buttermilk

1 egg

Makes 1 loaf

1. Preheat oven to 230°C/Gas Mark 8/450°F.
2. Grease a flat baking tin.
3. Combine dry ingredients. Make a little well and add honey, if using; then slowly add milk while mixing into flour with a fork. Add just enough milk that mixture comes together into a dough.
4. Knead briefly, then shape into round loaf. Place on baking tin and cut a cross all the way across the top and down the side with a sharp knife.
5. Brush top of loaves with beaten egg to which 1 Tbsp water has been added.
6. Bake for 15 minutes, then reduce heat to 180°C/Gas Mark 4/350°F and bake for another 15 minutes, or until done.

Variations
Add 1 tsp cinnamon or cardamom to dry ingredients.
Sprinkle top of loaf with sesame or poppy seeds.

Loving thanks to the Cluny bakers, whose energy shines through this section.

Shelley's Bagels

METRIC/IMPERIAL

680ml/24fl oz
potato cooking water
(or plain water)

2 Tbsp dry yeast

110-170g/4-6oz
honey

225g/8oz milk
powder

2 tsp salt

510g/18oz
wholemeal flour

510g/18oz
unbleached white
flour

110ml/4fl oz oil

1 egg

Makes 30 bagels

AMERICAN

3 cups potato
cooking water
(or plain water)

2 Tbsp dry yeast

⅓-½ cup honey

2 cups milk powder

2 tsp salt

4 cups whole wheat
flour

4 cups unbleached
white flour

½ cup oil

1 egg

Makes 30 bagels

1. Heat potato water to 32°C(90°F). Add yeast and honey to water and let stand for 5 minutes; then mix until dissolved.
2. Combine milk powder, salt and flours.
3. Add oil to yeast mixture, then gradually add flour mixture until dough is stiff. Add more flour if needed.
4. Turn dough onto floured board and knead for 10 minutes.
5. Let rise until double (about 1½ hours).
6. Punch down and knead again for a few minutes.
7. Roll out pieces of dough to 15cm x 2cm (6in x ¾ in). Bring ends around to form a circle. Pinch ends together, then smooth the seam.
8. Add 1 Tbsp sugar to 2 litres/3 pints/2 quarts boiling water.
9. Add bagels, a few at a time, to boiling water. They will sink to the bottom. When they rise to the top, turn over and continue to boil for 30 seconds.
10. Drain water, then place on greased baking sheet and brush with beaten egg.
11. Bake at 230°C/Gas Mark 8/450°F for 20 minutes, or until browned on both sides.

Variations
Maize meal (corn meal) can be used to replace ⅛ of the amount of either flour.
Before baking, top bagels with finely chopped onion, garlic,
sesame seeds, poppy seeds or coarse salt.

Honey Buns

METRIC/IMPERIAL

Sweet Roll Dough

2 Tbsp yeast

1 tsp honey

2 eggs

110ml/4fl oz oil

170g/6oz mild white honey

455ml/16fl oz warm water

60g/2oz milk powder

2 tsp salt

1kg/2 lbs 4oz wholemeal bread flour, or half wholemeal and half unbleached white

Filling

110g/4oz butter

170g/6oz honey

1 Tbsp cinnamon

85g/3oz raisins

Topping (Optional)

60g/2oz butter

85g/3oz honey

30g/1oz milk powder

¼ tsp vanilla

Makes 36 rolls

AMERICAN

Sweet Roll Dough

2 Tbsp yeast

1 tsp honey

2 eggs

½ cup oil

½ cup mild white honey

2 cups warm water

½ cup milk powder

2 tsp salt

8 cups whole wheat bread flour, or half whole wheat and half unbleached white

Filling

½ cup butter

½ cup honey

1 Tbsp cinnamon

½ cup raisins

Topping (Optional)

¼ cup butter

¼ cup honey

¼ cup milk powder

¼ tsp vanilla

Makes 36 rolls

---

1. Dissolve yeast in a small amount of warm (not hot) water. Add honey, and let mixture sit without stirring for 5 minutes, or until bubbly.
2. In a large bowl thoroughly beat together eggs, oil, honey, water, milk powder and salt.
3. Add the yeast and about half of the flour. With a wooden spoon and then by hand work in the remaining flour. Mix and knead adding as much flour as needed to keep dough from sticking. Knead for about 15 minutes, or until small bubbles begin to appear on surface of dough.
4. Cover with damp cloth and let rise in a warm place until double, about 1½ hours. Punch down and let rise again, about an hour.
5. For filling, slowly melt butter; when warm, remove from heat and whisk in honey and cinnamon. Mix well.
6. Divide dough in half. Roll each half out in a large rectangle, about 1cm(¼in) thick and 46cm(18in) long. Spread filling over all, then sprinkle raisins. Starting with long side, roll rectangle tightly, and seal edge by pinching. Cut each roll into 18 slices and place nine rolls each in four 20cm(8in) round baking tins. Let rise until double.
7. Bake at 190°C/Gas Mark 5/375°F for 20-25 minutes, or until browned.
8. Melt butter for topping. Remove from heat and whisk in remaining topping ingredients; mix well. When rolls have cooled, drizzle topping over them.
9. Optional: Sprinkle buns with chopped walnuts, slivered almonds or coconut.

Variations

The basic sweet roll dough can also be used for dinner rolls.
See *Shaping The Loaves* section for roll shapes and baking instructions.
For another breakfast roll, try Bill's Cardamom Buns. Follow steps 1-4 of the basic recipe, except add 2 Tbsp ground cardamom to the dough (it's especially tasty if the cardamom is freshly ground). After dough has risen twice, break off small pieces of dough and make a rope 25cm(10in) long and 1.5cm(½in) in diameter. Bring two ends together and pinch, making a shape like an oxen's yoke. Dip one surface of the roll first in melted butter, then in sugar. Place, sugar side up, on a greased baking tin. Let rise until puffy.
Bake at 210°C/Gas Mark 6/400°F for 20 minutes or until browned.

Bran Muffins

Serve with butter and cream cheese.

1. Pour boiling water over raisins to soak them. Set aside.
2. Preheat oven to 210°C/Gas Mark 6/400°F.
3. Grease muffin tins.
4. Mix dry ingredients together. Set aside.
5. Beat eggs, then add oil, honey, molasses and milk and mix thoroughly. (Honey and molasses will not stick to the measuring jug if oil has been measured in it first.)
6. Combine dry ingredients with molasses mixture. Just mix together; do not overbeat.
7. Drain raisins; fold them into batter.
8. Fill muffin tins two-thirds full with batter. Bake for 20-25 minutes, or until muffins spring back when pressed with a finger.

METRIC/IMPERIAL

225g/8oz raisins

510g/18oz soft wholemeal flour

140g/5oz bran

2½ tsp baking powder

2½ tsp bicarbonate of soda

1¼ tsp salt

3 eggs

170ml/6fl oz oil

170ml/6fl oz honey

170ml/6fl oz molasses

455ml/16fl oz milk

Makes 36 large muffins

AMERICAN

1½ cups raisins

4 cups whole wheat pastry flour

4 cups bran

3 tsp baking powder

3 tsp baking soda

1½ tsp salt

3 eggs

¾ cup oil

¾ cup honey

¾ cup molasses

2 cups milk

Makes 36 large muffins

Bobananda's Banana Muffins

No wheat, no sweet, no leavening.

1. Preheat oven to 210°C/Gas Mark 6/400°F.
2. Grease muffin tins.
3. Combine flours and salt. (Try grinding your own millet and rice flours.)
4. Mash bananas, then thoroughly mix bananas, egg yolks and oil.
5. Beat egg whites until stiff.
6. Lightly stir flour and banana mixtures together. Fold in raisins, then egg whites.
7. Spoon batter into muffin tins. Bake 20-25 minutes, or until browned.

METRIC/IMPERIAL

310g/11oz millet flour

60g/2oz rice flour

½ tsp salt

455g/1 lb bananas (weighed after peeling)

3 eggs, separated

110ml/4fl oz oil

140g/5oz raisins

Makes 18 large muffins

AMERICAN

2 cups millet flour

½ cup rice flour

½ tsp salt

2 cups mashed bananas

3 eggs, separated

½ cup oil

1 cup raisins

Makes 18 large muffins

Breakfasts

"But I always have an egg and toast for breakfast."
If you are looking for other options, here are some ideas.

Muesli

*Prepare muesli in bulk; then it's always ready
for a quick breakfast.*

METRIC/IMPERIAL

340g/11oz dried fruit
(such as apricots,
raisins, dates, figs,
sultanas or a mixture)

340g/11oz nuts
(such as walnuts,
cashews, almonds,
hazelnuts; use nuts
that are fresh)

455g/1 lb porridge
oats

85g/3oz wheat flakes

85g/3oz rye flakes

85g/3oz barley flakes

30g/1oz bran

30g/1oz coconut

60g/2oz sunflower
seeds

AMERICAN

2 cups dried fruit
(such as apricots,
raisins, dates, figs,
sultanas or a mixture)

2 cups nuts
(such as walnuts,
cashews, almonds,
hazelnuts; use nuts
that are fresh)

6 cups rolled oats

1 cup wheat flakes

1 cup rye flakes

1 cup barley flakes

¾ cup bran

¼ cup coconut

½ cup sunflower
seeds

1. Chop dried fruit. (To avoid a sticky knife when chopping fruit, first dip knife in solid butter.)
2. Mix all ingredients together and store in an airtight container.
3. Muesli is usually not cooked, but is eaten as is, topped with, for example, fresh fruit and milk, or apple purée and kefir.
4. To aid the digestibility of muesli, soak overnight in milk, water or apple juice.
5. If you are unable to obtain wheat, rye or barley flakes, substitute oats.

Granola

Granola is much like muesli, except that it is sweetened and roasted in the oven.

METRIC/IMPERIAL

140ml/5fl oz oil

340g/12oz honey

1½ tsp salt

1 tsp vanilla essence

680g/1½ lbs rolled oats

85g/3oz wheat flakes

85g/3oz rye flakes

85g/3oz barley flakes

200g/7oz nuts

85g/3oz sesame seeds

60g/2oz sunflower seeds

30g/1oz coconut

400g/14oz dried fruit

AMERICAN

1¼ cups oil

1 cup honey

1½ tsp salt

1 tsp vanilla

9 cups rolled oats

1 cup wheat flakes

1 cup rye flakes

1 cup barley flakes

1½ cups nuts

½ cup sesame seeds

½ cup sunflower seeds

¼ cup coconut

2½ cups dried fruit

1. Preheat oven to 210°C/Gas Mark 6/400°F.
2. With a whisk, mix together honey, oil, salt and vanilla.
3. Combine remaining ingredients except for dried fruit. Add oil-honey mixture to dry ingredients, but do not mix very much.
4. Pour into greased flat baking tins and bake for 30 to 60 minutes, stirring occasionally. While granola is baking, chop dried fruit; add it about 10 minutes before the end of baking. Granola is ready when golden brown and toasty. If you prefer granola that is sweeter, add more honey.
5. Cool completely, then store in an airtight container.
6. Serve with fresh fruit and yogurt.

Hot Cereal

Did you know that nearly any grain can be ground and used as a breakfast cereal? Some popular ones are rice, millet, corn, and a rice-millet mixture.

METRIC/IMPERIAL

680ml/24fl oz water

1 tsp salt

200g/7oz rice

Makes 4 servings

AMERICAN

3 cups water

1 tsp salt

1 cup rice

Makes 4 servings

1. Heat water and salt in the top of a double saucepan.
2. Meanwhile, grind rice in a grain grinder or a blender. It should be just a bit coarser than flour.
3. With a whisk, stir grain into water. Place over boiling water and cook for 20 minutes, or until tender. By cooking cereal in a double saucepan, cleaning the pan is a lot easier. Also, you don't have to watch over the cereal and stir it all the time; so you're free to make the rest of the breakfast or to take a shower.
4. Check the consistency of the cereal; add more water if needed. Cook another minute and serve.

Variations

For a very filling cereal, substitute milk for the water. To make these cereals for infants, use twice as much liquid. Whole grain cereal is very satisfying on its own, but if you'd like to add toppings, here are some ideas: *Sweet* nuts, dried fruit, fresh fruit, seeds, cinnamon, butter, honey. *Savoury* tamari, butter, steamed greens, sprouts.

Homemade Yogurt

METRIC/IMPERIAL

1 litre/2 pints milk

60g/2oz milk powder

1½ Tbsp plain yogurt (commercially prepared, or saved from your last batch)

AMERICAN

1 quart milk

½ cup milk powder

1½ Tbsp plain yogurt (commercially prepared, or saved from your last batch)

1. Be sure that all equipment used is very clean.
2. Heat milk to 75°C/170°F.
3. Blend powdered milk into milk. Adding powdered milk makes the yogurt thicker, and is a shortcut for the traditional method of heating milk for ½ hour.
4. Allow mixture to cool to 45°C/115°F, then add prepared yogurt and stir well. Do not succumb to the notion that if you use more starter, the yogurt will be thicker. In fact, there is a supersaturation point and the yogurt can be thinner.
5. Place yogurt in clean jars in a place where a temperature of 43°-48°C(110°-120°F) can be maintained. Too high a temperature will kill the bacteria and too low a temperature will not support growth. The shorter the incubation time (usually dependent on temperature), the sweeter the yogurt.
6. Yogurt is ready when it has become thick. That should take about four hours.
7. Yogurt is best when eaten within a day or two of being made. Folk wisdom says that the culture improves if it is used more often; so it's a good idea to make small batches and make it often. Refrigerate yogurt in covered container.

Yogurt Sundae

225ml/8fl oz yogurt

1 banana

1 Tbsp honey

4 Tbsp granola

140g/5oz fresh fruit in season

30g/1oz walnuts

30g/1oz raisins

1 Tbsp sunflower seeds

1 Tbsp grated coconut

Makes 1-2 servings

1. Spoon yogurt into a large dish. Slice banana over it, then drizzle honey and sprinkle on granola.
2. Slice fresh fruit and arrange over yogurt. Top with chopped walnuts, raisins, sunflower seeds and coconut. If you have a fresh strawberry, put it on the top.

1 cup yogurt

1 banana

1 Tbsp honey

4 Tbsp granola

1 cup fresh fruit in season

¼ cup walnuts

¼ cup raisins

1 Tbsp sunflower seeds

1 Tbsp grated coconut

Makes 1-2 servings

Kefir

Kefir is cultured, somewhat like yogurt; yet it has the advantage that it does not require heating, so it is a raw milk product.

Kefir is usually drunk rather than eaten. In order to make it, it is necessary to have kefir grains, which are obtainable at some whole food shops and also at the Cluny kitchen at Findhorn.

METRIC/IMPERIAL

1 litre/2 pints milk, preferably raw

½ tea cup kefir grains

AMERICAN

1 quart milk, preferably raw

½ cup kefir grains

1. Combine grains and milk in a perfectly clean jar.
2. Find a safe place to leave the jar at room temperature (21°C/70°F) for two to three days. Kefir is ready when the milk has thickened.
3. Pour kefir through a sieve. As kefir grains are damaged by contact with metal, use a plastic or wooden sieve. Stir kefir in the sieve (with a wooden spoon) until all the kefir has drained through and only grains are left. The kefir can be eaten immediately, or refrigerated for later use.
4. Wash grains under cold running water. Let them drain, then put in a clean jar and fill with milk for a new batch of kefir.

Some notes about kefir

1. If you must use pasteurised milk, strain the kefir grains and wash them daily.
2. For a thinner kefir, use fewer grains.
3. Kefir is milder when left for a shorter time. For a strong, almost alcoholic kefir, leave for seven days.
4. Kefir grains will multiply. Give some away to your friends.
5. Make a refreshing blender drink with kefir and fruit.

Fresh Fruit with Tahini Sauce

METRIC/IMPERIAL

Sauce

1 Tbsp tahini

1 tsp molasses

juice of 1 orange

Fruit

1 apple

1 banana

1 Tbsp dried fruit

1 Tbsp sunflower seeds

Makes 1 serving

AMERICAN

Sauce

1 Tbsp tahini

1 tsp molasses

juice of 1 orange

Fruit

1 apple

1 banana

1 Tbsp dried fruit

1 Tbsp sunflower seeds

Makes 1 serving

1. Mix all sauce ingredients together thoroughly.
2. Wash and chop fruits. Serve topped with sauce and sunflower seeds.

Variation
Use fresh fruits in season.

Eggs à la Moray Firth

METRIC/IMPERIAL

4 large tomatoes

salt and pepper

30g/1 oz Swiss cheese

30g/1 oz butter

4 eggs

parsley

Makes 4 servings

1. Preheat oven to 180°C/Gas Mark 4/350°F.
2. Grease baking dish.
3. Wash tomatoes; cut out stems and middle part.
4. Salt and pepper tomatoes.
5. Grate cheese and sprinkle half of it into the tomatoes.
6. Put tomatoes into baking dish. Into each one put a bit of butter, then break an egg into it. Salt the egg, sprinkle with remaining cheese, and top with a sprinkling of chopped parsley.
7. Bake for 20-25 minutes, or until eggs are cooked.

AMERICAN

4 large tomatoes

salt and pepper

¼ cup grated Swiss cheese

2 Tbsp butter

4 eggs

parsley

Makes 4 servings

Scrambled Tofu

METRIC/IMPERIAL

455g/1 lb tofu

1 onion

1 green pepper

2½ Tbsp oil

about 2 Tbsp tamari

1. Drain tofu well.
2. Peel and finely chop onion. Wash and finely chop green pepper.
3. Sauté onion and green pepper in oil.
4. When vegetables are completely tender, mix in tofu. As it is already cooked, it only needs to be heated through.
5. Add tamari to taste and serve immediately.

AMERICAN

2 cups tofu

1 onion

1 green pepper

3 Tbsp oil

about 2 Tbsp tamari

Baked Apples

METRIC/IMPERIAL

6 cooking apples

30g/1oz walnuts

30g/1oz currants

3 Tbsp honey or demerara sugar

30g/1oz soft flour

⅛ tsp ginger

½ tsp cinnamon

pinch of salt

drop of vanilla

1-2 Tbsp butter

yogurt (optional)

Makes 6 servings

AMERICAN

6 cooking apples

¼ cup walnuts

¼ cup currants

¼ cup honey or brown sugar

¼ cup pastry flour

⅛ tsp ginger

½ tsp cinnamon

pinch of salt

drop of vanilla

1-2 Tbsp butter

yogurt (optional)

Makes 6 servings

1. Preheat oven to 210°C/Gas Mark 6/400°F.
2. Wash and core apples; then make a slit around the middle (so that top can rise while baking).
3. Chop walnuts, mix with currants, honey, flour, ginger, cinnamon, salt and vanilla.
4. Melt butter and stir enough into mixture to moisten. Mix thoroughly.
5. Stuff mixture into apples.
6. Place apples in a greased baking dish and bake for 30-40 minutes, or until completely tender. Serve hot or cold. If you wish, top with yogurt.

Apple Purée

METRIC/IMPERIAL

5 cooking apples

4 whole cloves

1 cinnamon stick

1 tsp grated lemon rind

1 Tbsp butter

2 Tbsp honey or brown sugar (optional)

Makes 6 servings

AMERICAN

5 cooking apples

4 whole cloves

1 cinnamon stick

1 tsp grated lemon rind

1 Tbsp butter

2 Tbsp honey or brown sugar (optional)

Makes 6 servings

1. Wash, core and chop apples.
2. In a saucepan combine apples, cloves, cinnamon and lemon rind. Add enough water that apples can cook without sticking. Simmer apples until mushy, stirring occasionally.
3. If you wish, purée apples through a strainer.
4. Add butter and honey. Mix well.
5. Serve immediately, or store in a covered container in the refrigerator for later use.

Variation: APPLE SNOW
A quick and simple dessert, makes 8 servings

Instructions
1. Make apple purée using 4 Tbsp honey; let it cool.
2. Beat 2 egg whites until stiff; then fold into purée. Pour into serving dish.
3. Refrigerate for at least 2 hours before serving.

A Proper Tea Party

"Have some wine," the March Hare said in
an encouraging tone.
   Alice looked all round the table, but there was
nothing on it but tea. "I don't see any wine," she remarked.
   "There isn't any," said the March Hare.

'Alice in Wonderland' by Lewis Carroll

Michael Lindfield came to the pantry, looking for tea. I said that the tea was kept in the shed; only essential everyday items like eggs, milk and toilet paper were kept in the pantry. He drew himself up. "To an Englishman," he said, "tea is far more essential than toilet paper."

As traditional as the tea itself are the various cakes and sweets that accompany it. Here we have the full array, taken from recipe files   of some of the best bakers in the community.

Scottish Shortbread

METRIC/IMPERIAL

340g/12oz flour

225g/8oz butter
(no substitutes)

110g/4oz sugar

1. Preheat oven to 150°C/Gas Mark 1½-2/300°F.
2. Have butter at room temperature. Rub butter, sugar and flour together till it can be pressed into a ball.
3. On a board flatten the ball of dough to about 1.5cm(½in) thick. Cut into triangles or rectangles. Prick with a fork. Place on a baking tin and sprinkle with sugar.
4. Bake for 45 minutes, or until just beginning to turn golden around the edges.

AMERICAN

2½ cups flour

1 cup butter
(no substitutes)

½ cup sugar

Fairy Cakes

METRIC/IMPERIAL

110g/4oz margarine

110g/4oz castor sugar

2 eggs

170g/6oz plain flour

1½ tsp baking powder

¼ tsp salt

2 Tbsp milk

15 cake cases

1. Preheat oven to 220°C/Gas Mark 7/425°F.
2. Beat margarine and sugar together until smooth. Add eggs and mix thoroughly.
3. Sift together dry ingredients. Add dry ingredients and milk to batter. Beat well.
4. Spoon into paper cases and bake for 15-20 minutes, or until golden.

AMERICAN

½ cup margarine

⅔ cup sugar

2 eggs

1½ cups flour

2 tsp baking powder

¼ tsp salt

2½ Tbsp milk

15 muffin papers

Flap Jacks

METRIC/IMPERIAL

60g/2oz coconut

170g/6oz porridge oats

110g/4oz margarine

60g/2oz sugar

85g/3oz golden syrup

85g/3oz treacle

½ tsp salt

1. Preheat oven to 170°C/Gas Mark 3/335°F.
2. Mix coconut and oats together; set aside.
3. Gently melt margarine, sugar, syrup, treacle and salt together. If using metric or imperial measure, the saucepan can be put directly on the scale and quantities weighed in it, to avoid a treacle-syrup mess.
4. Add oats and coconut to margarine mixture; combine thoroughly.
5. Press into a greased 20cm(8in) square baking tin. Sprinkle a little more coconut and oats on top.
6. Bake for 30-35 minutes.
7. Remove from oven and cut into pieces immediately, but leave in tin until absolutely cold.

AMERICAN

⅔ cup coconut

1¾ cups rolled oats

½ cup margarine

⅓ cup sugar

¼ cup golden syrup or corn syrup

¼ cup treacle or light molasses

½ tsp salt

Butterscotch Biscuits

METRIC/IMPERIAL

570g/1 lb 4oz flour

¾ tsp bicarbonate of soda

¾ tsp salt

¾ tsp cinnamon

½ tsp cloves

½ tsp nutmeg

340g/12oz butter or margarine

185g/6½oz soft brown sugar

185g/6½oz white sugar

3 eggs, well beaten

130g/4½oz chopped walnuts *or* hazelnuts

1. Sift together flour, soda, salt, cinnamon, cloves and nutmeg. Set aside.
2. Cream together butter and sugars until smooth. Add egg and mix well.
3. Thoroughly mix in dry ingredients.
4. Stir in chopped nuts.
5. Make dough into a roll and wrap in grease-proof (waxed) paper. Chill overnight.
6. Slice, and bake on greased baking sheet at 180°C/ Gas Mark 4/350°F for 10 minutes.

AMERICAN

4½ cups flour

1 tsp baking soda

1 tsp salt

1 tsp cinnamon

½ tsp cloves

½ tsp nutmeg

1½ cups butter or margarine

1 cup light brown sugar

1 cup white sugar

3 eggs, well-beaten

1 cup chopped walnuts

Walnut Tarts

METRIC/IMPERIAL

Dough

85g/3oz cream cheese

110g/4oz butter or margarine

130g/4½oz flour

Filling

140g/5oz brown sugar

1 Tbsp soft butter

½ tsp vanilla

pinch of salt

1 egg, beaten

70g/2½oz walnuts, hazelnuts or pecans, coarsely cut

1. Let cream cheese and butter soften at room temperature, then mix together.
2. Stir in flour.
3. Chill dough for about one hour.
4. Shape into small balls; place in ungreased muffin tins and press dough into bottom and sides.
5. Prepare filling: beat together sugar, butter, vanilla and salt. Add egg and mix thoroughly.
6. Divide nuts in half. Sprinkle one half into bottoms of pastry cups; put a spoonful of filling in each cup; top with remaining nuts. Don't worry if it looks as though there isn't much filling in the tart. The filling expands as it bakes.
7. Bake at 170°C/Gas Mark 3/325°F for 25 minutes or until filling is set.
8. Allow to cool before removing from pans.

AMERICAN

Dough

6 Tbsp (3oz) cream cheese

½ cup butter or margarine

1 cup flour

Filling

¾ cup brown sugar

1 Tbsp soft butter

½ tsp vanilla

pinch of salt

1 egg, beaten

⅔ cup walnuts, hazelnuts or pecans, coarsely cut

Chocolate Chip Oat Cookies

METRIC/IMPERIAL

225g/8oz butter or margarine

185g/6½oz sugar

½ tsp vanilla

1 egg

255g/9oz flour

¾ tsp salt

¾ tsp baking powder

¾ tsp bicarbonate of soda

200g/7oz porridge oats

340g/12oz chocolate chips or plain chocolate, chopped small

60g/2oz chopped hazelnuts

AMERICAN

1 cup butter or margarine

1 cup sugar

1 tsp vanilla

1 egg

2 cups flour

1 tsp salt

1 tsp baking powder

1 tsp baking soda

2 cups oats

2 cups chocolate chips

½ cup chopped nuts

1. Preheat oven to 210°C/Gas Mark 6/400°F.
2. Grease a flat baking sheet.
3. Beat butter, sugar and vanilla until smooth and fluffy; mix in the egg.
4. Sift together flour, salt, baking powder and soda; stir into butter-sugar mixture.
5. Add oats and mix thoroughly.
6. Stir in chocolate chips and nuts.
7. Drop by spoonfuls onto baking sheet.
8. Bake for 10 minutes, or until lightly browned.

Date Wheels

METRIC/IMPERIAL

Dough

255g/9oz flour

¼ tsp salt

½ tsp bicarbonate of soda

110g/4oz butter or margarine

270g/9½oz soft brown sugar

1 egg, beaten

Filling

225g/8oz pitted dates

110ml/4fl oz water

1 tsp lemon juice

AMERICAN

Dough

2 cups flour

¼ tsp salt

½ tsp baking soda

½ cup butter or margarine

1½ cups light brown sugar

1 egg, beaten

Filling

1¼ cups pitted dates, packed tightly

½ cup water

1 tsp lemon juice

1. Sift together flour, salt and soda. Set aside.
2. Cream together butter, sugar and egg until completely smooth. Add dry ingredients and mix well.
3. Chill dough thoroughly.
4. Cut dates into pieces. Cook dates in a saucepan with water and lemon juice, just until ingredients are soft and well mushed together.
5. Let date mixture get completely cold.
6. Roll dough out into a large rectangle about 1cm(¼in) thick.
7. Spread date filling on the dough almost, but not quite, to the edge.
8. Roll up like a Swiss roll (jelly roll).
9. Wrap in grease-proof (waxed) paper and chill overnight, or freeze for later use.
10. When ready to bake, preheat oven to 180°C/Gas Mark4/ 350°F.
11. Slice wheels 1cm(¼in) thick.
12. Bake on greased baking sheets for about 8 minutes, or until lightly browned.

Ginger Cake

METRIC/IMPERIAL

110g/4oz margarine

110g/4oz soft brown sugar

110g/4oz golden syrup

200g/7oz plain flour

½ tsp salt

3 tsp ginger (or more, if you like a strong ginger taste)

1 tsp bicarbonate of soda

1 egg

140ml/5fl oz milk

1. Preheat oven to 160°C/Gas Mark 2/315°F.
2. Line a 18cm(7in) square baking tin with grease-proof (waxed) paper, after first rubbing it with margarine.
3. Melt margarine, sugar and syrup together in a saucepan.
4. Sift dry ingredients together, then add margarine-sugar mixture and mix thoroughly.
5. Beat egg and milk together, then stir into batter.
6. Pour batter into baking tin. Bake for 1½ hours, or until a fork inserted comes out clean.
7. Let cake cool, then cut into squares.

AMERICAN

½ cup margarine

⅔ cup light brown sugar

⅓ cup golden syrup *or* corn syrup

1¾ cups flour

½ tsp salt

4 tsp ginger (or more, if you like a strong ginger taste)

1¼ tsp baking soda

1 egg

½ cup milk

Coconut Pyramids

METRIC/IMPERIAL

1 large egg white

85g/3oz shredded coconut

85g/3oz castor sugar

½ tsp almond or vanilla essence

rice paper

85g/3oz plain chocolate

1. Preheat oven to 170°C/Gas Mark 3/325°F.
2. Mix coconut, sugar and essence together.
3. Beat egg white until stiff, then fold into coconut mixture.
4. Make tiny pyramids, then lay on a sheet of rice paper on an ungreased tin.
5. Bake for 15-20 minutes, or until browned. Cool on wire tray. Remove from rice paper. The rice paper, which is edible, will stick to the bottoms of the pyramids.
6. Melt chocolate in double saucepan, or in a glass bowl placed over boiling water. Dip base of each pyramid in chocolate. Set on wire tray to dry.

AMERICAN

1 large egg white

1 cup shredded coconut

½ cup white sugar

½ tsp almond or vanilla essence

rice paper

3 squares semi-sweet cooking chocolate

Kiftens

METRIC/IMPERIAL

400g/14oz butter

185g/6½oz sugar

1 tsp vanilla

140g/5oz shelled almonds

510g/18oz flour

110g/4oz icing sugar

1. Beat butter, sugar and vanilla together until fluffy.
2. Put almonds through fine grinder.
3. Alternate adding almonds and flour to butter-sugar mixture. Mix thoroughly.
4. Form little crescents and place on ungreased baking tin.
5. Bake at 180°C/Gas Mark 4/350°F for 15-20 minutes, or until lightly browned.
6. While still warm, roll in icing (powdered) sugar.

AMERICAN

1¾ cups butter

1 cup sugar

1 tsp vanilla

1 cup shelled almonds

4 cups flour

1 cup powdered sugar

Carob Nut Brownies

METRIC/IMPERIAL

110g/4oz butter or margarine

110g/4oz honey

60g/2oz brown sugar

1 egg

85g/3oz flour

60g/2oz carob powder

¾ tsp baking powder

½ tsp salt

½ tsp vanilla

130g/4½oz chopped walnuts, cashews or a mixture of the two

1. Preheat oven to 180°C/Gas Mark 4/350°F.
2. Grease a 20cm(8in) square baking tin.
3. Beat butter, honey and sugar together until smooth.
4. Stir in beaten egg.
5. Sift dry ingredients together, add to batter and mix thoroughly.
6. Add vanilla and chopped nuts.
7. Spoon into baking tin and bake for 30-35 minutes, or until a fork inserted comes out clean.
8. Cut into squares when cool.

AMERICAN

½ cup butter or margarine

⅓ cup honey

⅓ cup brown sugar

1 egg

⅔ cup flour

½ cup carob powder

1 tsp baking powder

½ tsp salt

1 tsp vanilla

1 cup chopped walnuts, cashews or a mixture of the two

Oatcakes

With brie and fruit, a complete snack.

METRIC/IMPERIAL

85g/3oz currants (optional)

190g/7oz porridge oats

130g/4½ oz oatmeal

130g/4½oz soft wholemeal flour

1 tsp salt

4 Tbsp oil

110ml/4fl oz water or liquid from soaking currants

1. Pour boiling water over currants. Set aside.
2. Preheat oven to 180°C/Gas Mark 4/350°F.
3. Rub a baking tin with butter.
4. Mix dry ingredients together, then add oil and mix thoroughly.
5. Drain currants, saving the liquid. Add currants to dough.
6. Add enough water so that ingredients hold together in a firm dough.
7. On a floured surface, roll dough out and cut into small rounds, 5cm(2in) in diameter.
8. Place on baking tin; bake for 15 minutes, or until cakes are beginning to brown.

AMERICAN

⅔ cup currants (optional)

2 cups rolled oats

1 cup oat flour

1 cup whole wheat pastry flour

1 tsp salt

⅓ cup oil

½ cup water or liquid from soaking currants

Currant Scones

Serve with whipped cream, butter and jam.

METRIC/IMPERIAL

40g/1½oz currants

280g/10oz flour

¾ tsp salt

½ tsp bicarbonate of soda

¾ tsp baking powder

85g/3oz butter or margarine

140ml/5fl oz (approximately) sour milk, buttermilk or kefir

AMERICAN

⅓ cup currants

2½ cups flour

¾ tsp salt

½ tsp baking soda

1 tsp baking powder

6 Tbsp butter or margarine

⅔ cup (approximately) sour milk, buttermilk or kefir

1. Preheat oven to 220°C/Gas Mark 7/425°F.
2. Pour enough boiling water over currants to cover them. Set aside.
3. Sift dry ingredients together.
4. Work butter into dry ingredients with fingers until the mixture resembles oats.
5. Drain water from currants and add them to the dough.
6. Add just enough milk so that dough can hold together when pressed into a ball.
7. On a floured surface pat dough out to about 2cm(¾in) thick. Cut fancy shapes or simple 5cm(2in) diameter circles.
8. Brush tops with milk and bake on an ungreased baking tin for 10-20 minutes, or until golden on top.
9. Serve immediately, wrapped in a cloth.

Variations

For cheese scones, omit currants and add 110g/4oz/1 cup grated cheddar cheese instead.
Brush tops of scones with beaten egg, then sprinkle with more grated cheese.
For plain scones, omit currants.

Cheese Straws

METRIC/IMPERIAL

225g/8oz flour

dash cayenne

½ tsp salt

½ tsp mustard powder

60g/2oz shortening

85g/3oz margarine

110g/4oz cheddar cheese, grated

170g/6oz parmesan cheese, grated

1 egg

AMERICAN

2 cups flour

dash cayenne

½ tsp salt

½ tsp mustard powder

¼ cup shortening

6 Tbsp margarine

1 cup grated cheddar cheese

1¾ cups grated parmesan cheese

1 egg

1. Sift together dry ingredients. Cut in shortening and margarine, then add remaining ingredients and mix thoroughly.
2. Roll out and cut in straws 1cm(¼in) wide.
3. Bake at 240°C/Gas Mark 9/475°F for 7-10 minutes, or until browned.

Desserts

"All festivals, truly conceived and manifested, are necessary
because in their own fashion they are part of the great rituals of life.
They are periods when people come together in blending
to create and release into the world the energies of upliftment
and effervescence, of laughter, song and dance."

David Spangler, Festivals in the New Age.

Desserts are a celebration. Birthdays, weddings, solstices, equinoxes, beginnings and endings all deserve special observances. In celebrating through food, we also celebrate our connection with the earth. What are the foods we eat at special times? Something as simple as the first raspberries of the season, served with cream, can be an elegant dessert. Or a pineapple, ripe and sweet, cut into chunks and served in its own shell. Or melon halves with the seed scooped out, then soured cream and blackberries piled into the centre. Unusual and different cheeses; each fruit as it comes into season. Then there are the all-out extravagances, the real splurges, using ingredients we wouldn't normally use in our day-to-day lives. Most of the recipes in this section fall into that category. Special ingredients, extra time spent, elaborate decoration, uncommon tastes; in these ways we recognise and celebrate the unforgettable events in our lives.

Isla's Cake

A truly unforgettable chocolate cake, created for Isla's blessing when she was a baby.

METRIC/IMPERIAL

Cake batter

390g/13oz sugar

225ml/8fl oz oil

2 eggs

85g/3oz unsweetened cocoa powder

400g/14oz flour

1 tsp bicarbonate of soda

225ml/8fl oz hot water

225ml/8fl oz sour milk

1 tsp vanilla

60g/2oz chopped walnuts

Filling

30g/1oz sugar

225g/8oz cream cheese

1 egg

½ tsp vanilla

45g/1½oz shredded coconut

225g/8oz semi-sweet chocolate chips or plain chocolate, chopped small

Icing

⅓ litre/½ pint whipping cream, whipped

AMERICAN

Cake batter

2 cups sugar

1 cup oil

2 eggs

¾ cup unsweetened cocoa powder

3 cups flour

1 tsp baking soda

1 cup hot water

1 cup sour milk

1 tsp vanilla

½ cup chopped walnuts

Filling

¼ cup sugar

8oz cream cheese

1 egg

½ tsp vanilla

½ cup shredded coconut

1 cup chocolate chips

Icing

1½ cups whipping cream, whipped

1. Preheat oven to 180°C/Gas Mark 4/350°F.
2. Rub a 23cm(9in) deep, removable-bottom baking tin with butter, then dust with flour. Set aside.
3. Mix sugar, eggs and oil together until smooth.
4. Sift dry ingredients together, then add to batter and mix well.
5. Add hot water and mix it in, then milk, and mix thoroughly.
6. Add vanilla and walnuts.
7. For filling, mix sugar and cream cheese until smooth; blend in egg and vanilla; finally, add coconut and chocolate chips.
8. Pour half the cake batter into baking tin.
9. Spread filling evenly over batter (as filling is quite thick, this will need to be done with your fingers or with spoons).
10. Carefully pour other half of cake batter over filling.
11. Bake for 70 minutes, or until done (when a fork inserted in top part of cake comes out clean).
12. Remove from oven and let cake remain in baking tin until cool, as the filling is very soft and must be completely cool to become solid. This will take several hours.
13. Carefully remove cake from tin.
14. Ice cake on top and sides with whipped cream.

Birthday Cake

METRIC/IMPERIAL

280ml/10fl oz boiling water

110g/4oz butter or margarine

100g/3½oz rolled oats

170g/6oz honey

185g/6½oz demerara sugar

185g/6½oz soft wholemeal flour

¾ tsp bicarbonate of soda

1 tsp cinnamon

¼ tsp salt

2 eggs

Topping

85g/3oz butter, melted

85g/3oz demerara sugar

85g/3oz shredded coconut

130g/4½oz chopped walnuts or hazelnuts

5 Tbsp cream or evaporated milk

AMERICAN

1¼ cups boiling water

½ cup butter or margarine

1 cup oatmeal

½ cup honey

1 cup light brown sugar

1½ cups whole wheat pastry flour

1 tsp baking soda

1 tsp cinnamon

¼ tsp salt

2 eggs

Topping

6 Tbsp butter, melted

½ cup light brown sugar

1 cup shredded coconut

1 cup chopped walnuts

6 Tbsp cream or evaporated milk

1. Pour boiling water over butter, oats and honey. Cover for 20 minutes.
2. Preheat oven to 180°C/Gas Mark 4/350°F.
3. Rub a 33 x 23 x 5cm (13 x 9 x 2in) baking tin with butter; then using a tea strainer dust with flour.
4. Sift dry ingredients together and set aside.
5. Stir oats mixture until thoroughly blended, then mix in beaten eggs.
6. Add dry ingredients and mix well.
7. Pour into baking tin. Bake for 45 minutes, or until a fork inserted comes out clean.
8. Mix topping ingredients together.
9. If the baking tin is also appropriate for serving, topping can be spread on warm cake, browned under grill (broiler), then left to cool until serving time.
10. If cake is to be removed to a separate serving platter, choose one that can withstand the heat of the grill. Allow cake to cool first, then remove to platter. Spread cake with topping and quickly brown under grill.

Swede Pie

The usual response to this pie is astonishment that the humble swede could taste so good. One person called it 'Swede Surprise'.

METRIC/IMPERIAL

Crust

40g/1½oz rolled oats

55g/2oz wholemeal flour

30g/1oz freshly ground hazelnuts, or any other nut or seed

1½ Tbsp demerara sugar

½ tsp cinnamon

½ tsp salt

55g/2oz butter

1½ Tbsp oil

2 Tbsp water

Filling

225g/8oz swede (weighed after peeling)

140ml/5fl oz cooking water

140ml/5fl oz milk

2 Tbsp cornflour

85g/3oz demerara sugar

¼ tsp salt

1 tsp cinnamon

1 tsp nutmeg

1 tsp fresh chopped lemon balm (if available)

3 eggs

140ml/5fl oz whipping cream

AMERICAN

Crust

½ cup oatmeal

½ cup whole wheat pastry flour

¼ cup ground walnuts, or any other nut or seed

2 Tbsp light brown sugar

½ tsp cinnamon

½ tsp salt

4 Tbsp butter

2 Tbsp oil

2 Tbsp water

Filling

1 medium swede (rutabaga): 1¼ cups when chopped and cooked

½ cup cooking water

½ cup milk

2 Tbsp cornstarch

½ cup light brown sugar

¼ tsp salt

1 tsp cinnamon

1 tsp nutmeg

1 tsp fresh chopped lemon balm (if available)

3 eggs

1 cup whipping cream

Crust

1. Preheat oven to 220°C/Gas Mark 7/425°F.
2. Mix dry ingredients together.
3. Cut in butter until well blended.
4. Mix oil in with a fork.
5. Add as much water as needed to hold pastry together.
6. Press into 23cm(9in) round pie dish.
7. Bake for 10 minutes or until brown.
8. Allow pastry to cool before filling.

Filling

1. Wash, peel and chop swedes. Cook in small amount of boiling water until soft. Drain and save cooking water.
2. Heat milk and cooking water to just under boiling point.
3. Put swedes, cornflour, sugar, salt, cinnamon, nutmeg, cooking water, milk and lemon balm in blender. Blend until smooth.
4. Cook mixture in top of double saucepan, or in a bowl over boiling water, until it thickens. Cover and continue to cook another 10 minutes.
5. Separate eggs. Set whites aside. Beat egg yolks.
6. Add a few spoonfuls of swede mixture to egg yolks.
7. Return egg yolk mixture to saucepan and continue cooking for 2 minutes.
8. Remove from heat and allow to cool.
9. When mixture has cooled, beat egg whites until stiff.
10. Gently fold egg whites into swede mixture. Pour into baked crust.
11. Refrigerate for at least two hours.
12. Before serving, whip cream and spread over top of pie.

Variations

In place of swedes use another vegetable, such as pumpkin, squash or parsnips.
This recipe was originally made with turnips and was a resounding success,
although we decided later that it tasted a bit too 'turnippy'.

Shortcrust Pastry

METRIC/IMPERIAL

250g/8oz flour

¾ tsp salt

60g/2oz butter

60g/2oz vegetable
shortening

5-6 Tbsp ice water

*Makes one 20cm (8in)
double-crust pie, or
two single-crust pies*

1. Mix flour and salt.
2. Blend butter and shortening together thoroughly.
3. Cut butter-shortening mixture into flour, using a pastry blender or fingers until mixture resembles rolled oats.
4. Mix in ice water with a fork, one Tbsp at a time, using just enough water for dough to be gathered up in a ball.
5. If filling and crust are to be baked together, dough is now ready to be used. For a prebaked pastry shell, continue with steps 6 to 9.
6. Roll dough out; fit into baking dish; trim edges. Prick bottom and sides with a fork.
7. Place in refrigerator for one hour.
8. Preheat oven to 230°C/Gas Mark 8/450°F.
9. Remove crust from refrigerator and bake immediately for 10-12 minutes or until golden brown.

AMERICAN

2 cups flour

1 tsp salt

⅓ cup butter

⅓ cup vegetable
shortening

5-6 Tbsp ice water

*Makes one 20cm (8in)
double-crust pie, or
two single-crust pies.*

Suggestions

Shortcrust pastry can be mixed in advance, and left in the refrigerator for up to one week.
For ease in handling, it should be removed from refrigerator one hour before rolling out.
Margarine, butter and vegetable shortening can be used interchangeably although, for the
beginner, margarine or vegetable shortening is easier to work with. After you are
comfortable with mixing and rolling dough, use half butter for added flavour.
The amount of salt needed will vary according to the type of shortening used.
Handle the dough as little as possible. Mix it and roll it out quickly.
Don't despair if your first crust is a bit odd. Experience brings better results.

Fresh Berry Pie

METRIC/IMPERIAL

One single-crust pie
shell, prebaked (see
recipe for Shortcrust
Pastry)

500g/18oz fresh
blackberries, straw-
berries or raspberries

3 Tbsp cornflour

170g/6oz sugar *or*
340g/12oz mild
honey

¼ tsp salt

140ml/5fl oz
whipping cream

1. Wash and drain the berries.
2. Mash half the berries.
3. Mix cornflour, sugar and salt in a medium-sized saucepan.
4. Add mashed berries to cornflour mixture and cook until mixture becomes thick and clear.
5. Place remaining unmashed berries in the baked pie shell.
6. Pour hot berry mixture over fresh berries.
7. Cool. Refrigerate for at least one hour.
8. Top with whipped cream.

AMERICAN

One single-crust pie
shell, prebaked (see
recipe for Shortcrust
Pastry)

4 cups fresh black-
berries, strawberries
or raspberries

3 Tbsp cornstarch

1 cup sugar or mild
honey

¼ tsp salt

1 cup whipping
cream

Homemade Apple Pie

METRIC/IMPERIAL

Shortcrust Pastry for one double-crust pie, made with 84% wholemeal flour

900g/2 lbs cooking apples

2 Tbsp butter or margarine

2 Tbsp flour

3 Tbsp brown sugar *or*

2 Tbsp honey

juice of ½ lemon

1½ tsp cinnamon

½ tsp ground cloves

⅛ tsp ground cardamom

1 egg

Makes 8-12 servings

AMERICAN

Shortcrust Pastry for one double-crust pie, made with whole wheat pastry flour

2 lbs cooking apples

2 Tbsp butter or margarine

2 Tbsp flour

3 Tbsp brown sugar *or* 2 Tbsp honey

juice of ½ lemon

1½ tsp cinnamon

½ tsp ground cloves

⅛ tsp ground cardamon

1 egg

Makes 8-12 servings

1. Preheat oven to 180°C/Gas Mark 4/350°F.
2. Wash and core apples; slice thin.
3. Cut butter into small pieces. Mix apples, butter, flour, sugar, lemon juice and spices; stir until well mixed. Set this mixture aside while preparing the pastry.
4. Divide shortcrust pastry in half. Roll out half and fit into a large, round, glass pie dish (23cm/9in).
5. Taste the apple mixture and add more honey, lemon or spices if needed (apples differ greatly in flavour), then put apples into pie dish.
6. Roll out other half of pastry and cut strips about 2cm(¾in) wide.
7. Lay these strips of dough across dish to make a lattice top (as in weaving).
8. Turn up pastry hanging over edge of pan, thus forming a ridge of dough around pan, blending all the ends of the lattice. Flute the edge around the pan.
9. Prepare an egg wash by beating an egg with 1 Tbsp water or milk, then brush dough with it. (Leftover egg can be used in other cooking.)
10. Bake pie for one hour, or until crust is golden brown and apples are tender when pierced.

Serving Suggestions

Serve warm with whipped cream, vanilla ice cream or cheddar cheese.

This pie is wholesome and filling: the perfect complement to a light meal or brunch, practically a meal in itself when served for tea.

Variation

Add walnuts, sunflower seeds or any nut or seed to the apple mixture.

Chocolate Cream Pie

METRIC/IMPERIAL

One 20cm(8in)
single-crust pie shell,
prebaked (see recipe
for Shortcrust Pastry)

5 Tbsp unsweetened
cocoa powder

125g/4½oz sugar

5 Tbsp cornflour

⅛ tsp salt

700ml/1¼ pints milk

½ tsp vanilla

½ tsp grated orange
rind (optional)

140ml/5fl oz
whipping cream

Makes 8 servings

AMERICAN

One 8in single-crust
pie shell, prebaked
(see recipe for
Shortcrust Pastry)

6 Tbsp unsweetened
cocoa powder

¾ cup sugar

6 Tbsp cornstarch

⅛ tsp salt

3 cups milk

½ tsp vanilla

½ tsp grated orange
rind (optional)

1 cup whipping
cream

Makes 8 servings

1. Combine cocoa powder, sugar, cornflour and salt in a
   glass bowl or in the top of a double saucepan.
2. Add milk and mix thoroughly.
3. Place over pan of boiling water. Cook for about 10
   minutes, stirring constantly. When it thickens, cover and
   cook for 10 minutes more.
4. Remove from heat. When slightly cooled, add vanilla and
   orange rind.
5. Pour into prebaked pie shell.
6. Cool, then refrigerate for at least two hours.
7. Top with whipped cream before serving.

Banana Cream Pie

METRIC/IMPERIAL

One 20cm(8in) single-crust pie shell, prebaked (see recipe for Shortcrust Pastry)

3 Tbsp cornflour

⅛ tsp salt

½ litre/1 pint milk

4 Tbsp mild honey

1 egg, well-beaten

1 banana

½ tsp. vanilla

140ml/5fl oz whipping cream

Makes 6-8 servings

AMERICAN

One 8in single-crust pie shell, prebaked (see recipe for Shortcrust Pastry)

3 Tbsp cornstarch

⅛ tsp salt

2 cups milk

¼ cup mild honey

1 egg, well-beaten

1 banana

½ tsp vanilla

1 cup whipping cream

Makes 6-8 servings

1. Combine cornflour (cornstarch), salt and milk in a glass bowl or in the top of a double saucepan. Mix thoroughly.
2. Place over pan of boiling water. When mixture begins to get warm, add honey.
3. Continue cooking, stirring constantly, for about 10 minutes, or until mixture begins to thicken. Cover and cook for another 10 minutes.
4. In a separate bowl, stir 8 Tbsp of the thickened mixture into one well-beaten egg. Return this mixture to saucepan and blend thoroughly.
5. Continue to cook for another two minutes, stirring constantly.
6. Remove from heat. Allow to cool slightly.
7. While mixture is cooling, peel and slice banana into pie shell.
8. Stir vanilla into thickened milk mixture.
9. Pour mixture over banana in pie shell.
10. Allow pie to cool, then refrigerate for at least two hours.
11. Top with whipped cream before serving.

Variation

For a coconut cream pie, omit banana and add 90g/3oz/1 cup freshly grated coconut to the thickened milk mixture just before pouring into pie shell. Top with whipped cream.

Chocolate Leaves

An after-dinner mint introduced to us by Maggie Miller of Newbold House.

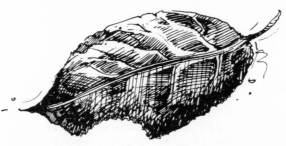

METRIC/IMPERIAL

100g/3.5oz chocolate

few drops peppermint flavouring

Serves 8 people, 3 or 4 leaves each.

AMERICAN

3.5oz chocolate

few drops peppermint flavouring

Serves 8 people, 3 or 4 leaves each.

1. Pick rose leaves; choose leaves that are smooth and of different sizes for variety.
2. Break into individual leaves; wash and dry each one.
3. Slowly melt chocolate in the top of a double saucepan or in a glass bowl over simmering water. Do not boil water.
4. When chocolate is melted, remove pan from heat and add a few drops of peppermint flavouring. Taste to see that the amount is right.
5. Hold rose leaf vein side up.
6. Apply a thin coat of chocolate to leaf, using the handle of a wooden spoon. Spread chocolate to the edges, but do not allow to overflow to other side.

7. Gently put leaves on grease-proof (waxed) paper. Allow to set for 20-60 minutes, or until the leaf can be pulled away from the chocolate. The time varies greatly with the temperature of the kitchen. If the kitchen is too warm, the leaves may need to go into the refrigerator for a few minutes. But for greatest ease in pulling leaf away, don't allow chocolate to become totally hard.
8. Separate the rose leaf from the chocolate leaf, carefully and quickly, before the heat of the hand warms the chocolate. If bits of the leaf stick, use the point of a small knife to loosen them.

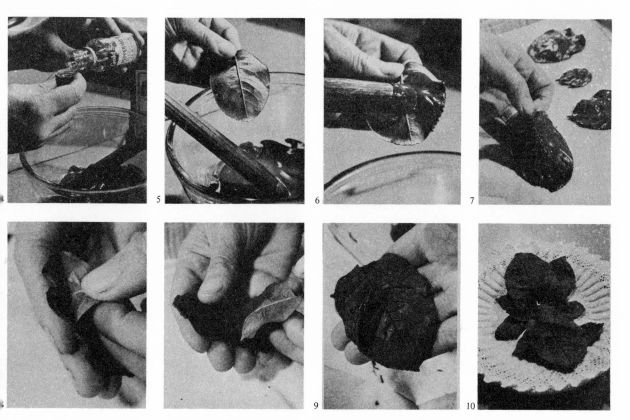

9. Set finished product in a cool place until serving time.
10. Arrange leaves on a plate, patterned side up.
11. Serve as an after-dinner mint.

Variations

In place of peppermint flavouring, use a flavoured liqueur or grated orange rind.
Use leaves as decoration for another dessert.

Traditional English Sherry Trifle

METRIC/IMPERIAL

Madeira Cake

225g/8oz plain flour

1 tsp baking powder

⅛ tsp salt

170g/6oz butter or margarine

170g/6oz sugar

3 eggs

Fillings

85g/3oz red jam

400g/14oz tin sliced peaches, pineapples or strawberries

2 bananas

340ml/12fl oz cream sherry (approximately)

AMERICAN

Madeira Cake

1¾ cups white flour

1 tsp baking powder

⅛ tsp salt

¾ cup butter or margarine

1 cup sugar

3 eggs

Fillings

½ cup red jam

14oz can sliced peaches, pineapples or strawberries

2 bananas

1½ cups cream sherry (approximately)

Madeira Cake

Note: The cake for the trifle must be baked 3-7 days ahead of time. The trifle is better if it is refrigerated for several hours before serving.

1. Preheat oven to 170°C/Gas Mark 3/325°F.
2. Rub a 23 x 12 x 7cm (9 x 5 x 2½in) baking tin with butter, then dust with flour.
3. Sift together flour, baking powder and salt. Set aside.
4. Cream together the butter and sugar.
5. Add beaten eggs, then mix thoroughly.
6. Blend in flour mixture until smooth. Pour into baking tin.
7. Bake for 1¼ hours or until done. Remove from pan.
8. Set cake in a safe place and allow it to become stale (3-7 days).

Filling

1. Drain juice from tinned fruit.
2. Slice cake and spread pieces with jam. Sandwich it. Cut into smaller pieces and fit in bottom of a large bowl, preferably glass, or use three small bowls.
3. Spoon sherry over the cake, just to soak cake but not make it mushy.
4. Arrange fruit on cake with sliced bananas.

Custard

1 litre/2 pints milk

6 Tbsp sugar

6 eggs

½ tsp vanilla

Topping

¼ litre/½ pint
whipping cream
(more if you wish to
be extravagant)

60g/2oz glacé
cherries

30g/1oz toasted
almond flakes

Makes 20 servings

Custard

1. Heat milk. (Do not allow to boil.)
2. Beat eggs vigorously for one minute.
3. Into the top of a double saucepan, or a glass bowl, pour the milk through a strainer (to remove any skin that may have formed on the surface).
4. Pour eggs through the strainer into the milk. Stir in sugar.
5. Place pan over boiling water. Be sure that the bottom of the pan holding the custard does not touch the boiling water, but is suspended over it.
6. Cook mixture until it begins to thicken and will coat the back of a wooden spoon (10-15 minutes).
7. Remove from heat and add vanilla.
8. Immerse custard pan in cold water to speed cooling time. Change water if necessary.
9. Stir custard occasionally as it is cooling. Custard will thicken somewhat as it cools.
10. When custard has cooled, pour over the trifle to form a smooth layer on top.
11. Refrigerate for several hours or overnight.

Topping

1. Whip cream and spread over custard.
2. Cut cherries in half. Decorate the top with almonds and cherries.
3. Refrigerate until serving time.

Custard

4 cups milk

6 Tbsp sugar

6 eggs

½ tsp vanilla

Topping

1 cup whipping cream
(more if you wish to
be extravagant)

½ cup candied
cherries

¼ cup toasted
almond flakes

Makes 20 servings

Variations
Use fresh fruit or berries in place of tinned.
The trifle can be made in a single day if you purchase a cake which is already stale.

Banana Date Nut Wedding Cake

9 eggs, room temperature

1kg/2 lb 4oz 84% flour *or*

mixture of 84% and unbleached white

1 tsp salt

28g/1oz bicarbonate of soda *or*

half bicarbonate of soda and half baking powder

1 tsp cinnamon

½ tsp nutmeg

¼ tsp ginger

½ tsp cloves

400ml/14fl oz safflower oil

840g/1lb 14oz honey

1.68kg/3 lb 12oz mashed bananas, weighed after peeling (approximately 20 bananas)

455g/1 lb finely chopped dates

455g/1 lb walnuts, finely chopped

Icing

6 oranges

900g/2 lbs butter or margarine

1.37kg/3 lbs honey

455g/1 lb milk powder

1 tsp vanilla

fresh flowers

Makes 50 generous servings (1 large sheet cake)

Cake

1. Preheat oven to 170°C/Gas Mark 4/350°F.
2. Lightly oil and thoroughly flour a large sheet pan. (Or two pans, each 48 x 38 x 4cm [19 x 15 x 1½in].)
3. Break eggs into mixer bowl and begin whisking at moderate speed.
4. Meanwhile sift all dry ingredients together and set aside.
5. When eggs are whipped and frothy, pour oil in slowly and continue whipping.
6. When eggs and oil are well mixed, stop mixer and pour honey in. Reduce speed and whip more. (Chop dates and nuts in the meantime.)
7. When liquid is well mixed, reduce speed and gradually add flour and mashed bananas alternately. You may need to stop mixing occasionally, to scrape bottom of bowl.
8. When batter is well mixed, add walnuts and dates. Mix one or two minutes, then give whole mix one final whip at high speed.
9. Turn into baking pan.
10. Bake for about 40 minutes, or until golden brown. (Knife inserted will come out clean.)
11. Cool well in pan.
12. To remove cake from pan, loosen edges with a knife, then place another pan the same size on top of cake, and holding firmly the sides of the pans, flip cake over. Now bottom will be showing. Next, place the serving platter over the cake and repeat the flipping procedure. The cake will now be right side up.
13. Tuck strips of greaseproof paper (waxed paper) under the edges of the cake so that the serving platter will remain clean while cake is being iced.

Icing

1. Grate orange rind; then juice oranges. Set grated rind and juice aside.
2. In a mixer, whip butter.
3. Add honey and mix until well blended.
4. Sift in milk powder, add orange juice, grated rind and vanilla; mix thoroughly.
5. Ice cake when completely cool. Decorate with flowers.

9 eggs, room temperature

8 cups whole wheat pastry flour *or*

mixture of whole wheat pastry and unbleached white

1 tsp salt

5 tsp baking soda *or*

half baking soda and half baking powder

1 tsp cinnamon

½ tsp nutmeg

¼ tsp ginger

½ tsp cloves

1¾ cups safflower oil

2½ cups honey

7½ cups mashed bananas (approximately 20 bananas)

3 cups finely chopped dates

3½ cups finely chopped walnuts

Icing

6 oranges

4 cups butter or margarine

4 cups honey

4 cups milk powder

1 tsp vanilla

fresh flowers

Makes 50 generous servings (1 large sheet cake)

Vadan's Frozen Yogurt Pie

METRIC/IMPERIAL

Crust

125g/5oz granola digestive biscuits, crushed fine

30g/1oz walnuts or cashews, finely chopped

1 tsp cinnamon

dash of cloves

dash of allspice

85g/3oz melted butter

Filling

450g/1lb cream cheese

225ml/8fl oz yogurt

50g/2oz milk powder

grated rind of a lemon

½ tsp vanilla

2 bananas, mashed

honey to taste (about 2 Tbsp)

140g/5oz fresh fruit (berries or pineapple are nice)

½ banana, a few berries, mint leaves for decoration

AMERICAN

Crust

1½ cups honey graham crackers, crushed fine

¼ cup walnuts or cashews, finely chopped

1 tsp cinnamon

dash of cloves

dash of allspice

6 Tbsp melted butter

Filling

2 cups cream cheese

1 cup yogurt

½ cup milk powder

grated rind of a lemon

1 tsp vanilla

2 bananas, mashed

honey to taste (about 2 Tbsp)

1 cup fresh fruit (berries or pineapple are nice)

½ banana, a few berries, mint leaves for decoration

This is the perfect dessert for a hot summer's night. Should one of these ever come to Northern Scotland, we are prepared!

Crust

1. Preheat oven to 150°C/Gas Mark 2/300°F.
2. Mix dry ingredients together.
3. Add melted butter and mix thoroughly.
4. Into a 23cm(9in) deep pie dish press crust mixture evenly with fingers.
5. Bake for 15 minutes. Cool thoroughly before filling.

Filling

1. Soften cream cheese with a spoon, then whisk together with yogurt.
2. Sift milk powder in and mix thoroughly.
3. Add lemon rind, vanilla and mashed bananas; stir until blended.
4. Add honey and mix well.
5. Gently fold in other fresh fruit. If using small berries, leave them whole. Pineapple or other fruit must be chopped into small chunks.
6. Pour mixture into pie crust.
7. Vadan says: "My favourite part (other than eating it) is decorating it. I usually intersperse banana slices with berries around the edges and make a mandala with fresh mint leaves and perhaps a strawberry in the centre."
8. Thoroughly freeze pie (overnight).
9. When ready to serve, remove from freezer and allow to thaw for 30-45 minutes before cutting. (If you have a very cold freezer, allow more time for thawing.)

Very Chocolate Cake

We dedicate this cake to David Spangler,
the world's greatest chocolate fan.

METRIC/IMPERIAL

110g/4oz bitter chocolate *or*

2½oz cocoa powder

110g/4oz butter (or 220g/8oz, if cocoa is used)

¼ litre/½ pint boiling water

370g/13oz sugar

255g/9oz flour

7 Tbsp sour milk

¼ tsp bicarbonate of soda

2 beaten eggs

2 tsp vanilla

Icing

270g/9½oz sugar

90g/3oz bitter chocolate *or*

7 Tbsp cocoa

¼ litre/½pint cream

1 Tbsp butter

½ tsp vanilla

Cake Instructions

1. Preheat oven to 180°C/Gas Mark 4/350°F.
2. Rub two round cake pans with butter, then dust with flour.
3. Pour boiling water over chocolate and butter. Cover and let melt.
4. Add sugar and mix thoroughly.
5. Blend flour in lightly.
6. Mix sour milk and soda together, then add to batter.
7. Add eggs and vanilla; stir until batter is thoroughly blended.
8. Pour into baking pans.
9. Bake for 30 minutes or until done.
10. Let cake cool about 5 minutes, then remove from pan and let cool completely before icing.

Icing Instructions

1. In a saucepan, mix all ingredients together except vanilla.
2. Boil until soft ball forms when a small amount of icing is dropped in a dish of cold water.
3. Add vanilla
4. Allow icing to cool before applying.

Optional — sprinkle chopped walnuts on top.

AMERICAN

4 squares bitter chocolate, grated *or*

¾ cup cocoa powder

¼ cup butter (or ½ cup, if cocoa is used)

1 cup boiling water

2 cups sugar

2 cups flour

½ cup sour milk

1½ tsp baking soda

2 beaten eggs

2 tsp vanilla

Icing

1½ cups sugar

3 squares bitter chocolate *or*

9 Tbsp cocoa

1 cup cream

1 Tbsp butter

½ tsp vanilla

Cheesecake

METRIC/IMPERIAL

Crust

110g/4oz digestive biscuits, crushed fine

50g/2oz butter, melted

Filling

225g/8oz cream cheese

6½ Tbsp mild, white honey

1 Tbsp lemon juice

½ tsp vanilla

⅛ tsp salt

2 eggs, beaten

Topping

¼ litre/½ pint soured cream

2 Tbsp honey

½ tsp vanilla

1. Preheat oven to 160°C/Gas Mark 3/325°F.
2. Mix crumbs and butter together thoroughly, then press into a 20cm(8in) shallow baking tin, forming an even crust with your fingers.
3. Beat cream cheese until fluffy.
4. Blend in eggs.
5. Add honey, lemon juice, vanilla and salt; mix thoroughly.
6. Pour into pie crust and bake 25 to 30 minutes, or until set.
7. While pie is baking, mix topping ingredients together.
8. Pour topping over hot pie, and return to oven for an additional 10 minutes.
9. Cool, then chill for at least 8 hours.

AMERICAN

Crust

1¼ cups graham cracker crumbs

¼ cup butter, melted

Filling

1 cup (8oz) cream cheese

8 Tbsp mild, white honey

1 Tbsp lemon juice

½ tsp vanilla

⅛ tsp salt

2 eggs, beaten

Topping

1 cup sour cream

2 Tbsp honey

½ tsp vanilla

Cooked Pears

I enjoy ending an especially elaborate meal with two desserts. Cooked pears are an ideal first dessert course, as they are light and they clean the palate. The next dessert then seems to be all the more delicious.

METRIC/IMPERIAL

One half, firm, unripe pear per person

For each ½ litre/ 1 pint of water use 4 Tbsp demerara sugar or honey and ¼ tsp vanilla

1. Wash pears. Leave whole.
2. Put pears in pan and add just enough water to immerse them halfway.
3. Remove pears from water. Measure water.
4. Bring water to boil. Then carefully add pears.
5. Reduce heat and simmer until almost tender (about 10 minutes).
6. Add sugar or honey and continue simmering until pears can be easily pierced with a fork but are not mushy. Taste syrup and add more sweetener if needed.
7. Remove from heat and add vanilla.
8. Allow pears to cool slightly, then split in half. Serve each half in a bowl, cut side down, with some syrup spooned over.

AMERICAN

One half, firm, unripe pear per person

For each 2 cups of water use ¼ cup brown sugar or honey and ¼ tsp vanilla

Variations

Add cinnamon, cloves, nutmeg. Use other fruits, such as peaches or apricots.
If this is the only dessert being served, leave the pear whole and serve one per person.

Crème Caramel

METRIC/IMPERIAL

55g/2oz sugar

455ml/16fl oz milk

4 eggs

6 Tbsp sugar or mild honey

½ tsp vanilla

⅛ tsp salt

Makes 6-8 servings

1. Clean and dry thoroughly a 1 litre/2 pint/1 quart fancy baking mould. Set aside.
2. Preheat oven to 160°C/Gas Mark 2/325°F.
3. Slowly heat sugar in a heavy saucepan, stirring constantly, until sugar turns to syrup and becomes caramel-coloured.
4. Pour syrup into baking mould. Tilt mould around so that syrup covers as much of the surface as possible. Be careful, as the syrup is very hot. Set mould aside to cool.
5. Pour *boiling* water slowly and carefully into the hot caramel saucepan. (It will spit and steam, due to high temperature.) Stir water around, so that caramel won't stick. By doing this immediately the saucepan will be much easier to clean afterwards.
6. Beat eggs. Set aside.
7. In a saucepan, heat milk slightly. Remove from heat.
8. Add sugar; mix until dissolved.
9. Add beaten eggs, vanilla and salt; blend thoroughly.
10. Pour into baking mould.
11. Set mould inside larger dish of hot water in oven. (It is a bit tricky getting the baking mould in and out of a pan of hot water in the oven, but it is definitely worth it for the result of better texture.)
12. Bake for 40-60 minutes, or until a knife inserted in the centre comes out clean.
13. Cool, then refrigerate for several hours.
14. Just before serving, unmould the dessert. First loosen the edges with a knife, then place serving platter upside down over mould. Holding mould and platter securely together, quickly flip the dessert over. Remove mould. The caramel will now be a sauce on top of the dessert.

Variations
Decorate with flowers. Serve with whipped cream on the side.
Sprinkle with roasted cashews or almonds, chopped.

AMERICAN

8 Tbsp sugar

2 cups milk

4 eggs

½ cup sugar or mild honey

½ tsp vanilla

⅛ tsp salt

Makes 6-8 servings

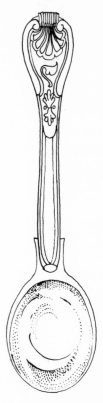

More than just a Croquembouche

The Croquembouche, a traditional French wedding cake, is a pile of cream-filled puffs held together by caramelised sugar. The wedding cake pictured here, the creation of Ike and Maggie Isaksen, began at Findhorn several years ago as a croquembouche, and now, many weddings later, has evolved to its present cake-filled form.

It appears to be much more difficult to make than it actually is. On the following pages we have presented the recipes for the various parts, then instructions for assembling the whole cake.

If you do not have access to the large equipment mentioned, divide the recipes in half or in fourths and use the equipment you have on hand.

It will take three amateur cooks about eight hours to make this cake. Plan to do the final assembly in the same place where the cake is to be served, as it cannot easily be moved.

If you prefer a cake made with whole foods, use your favourite cake recipe and follow the same procedure for assembling the cake.

This recipe makes 100 servings.

Filling

METRIC/IMPERIAL

670g/24oz castor sugar

20 egg yolks

340g/12oz plain flour

1.8 litres/3 pints milk

60g/2oz butter

¼ litre/½ pint cognac

grated rind of two oranges

grated rind of two lemons

AMERICAN

4 cups granulated sugar

20 egg yolks

2 cups white flour

8 cups milk

4 Tbsp butter

1 cup cognac

grated rind of two oranges

grated rind of two lemons

This filling may be made up to a week ahead of time, and kept refrigerated.

1. In a large, heavy saucepan or soup pot, whisk sugar and egg yolks until the mixture becomes pale yellow and can form a slowly dissolving ribbon when whisk is raised from mixture.
2. Add flour and mix thoroughly.
3. Bring milk to a boil. Very slowly pour milk into egg-sugar mixture, beating constantly.
4. Put saucepan over moderate heat, preferably over an asbestos mat, or a heat spreader, to avoid burning. Bring to a gentle boil, alternately beating with a wire whisk and stirring the bottom and sides of the pan with a wooden spoon. The filling needs constant attention at this point, to avoid lumping or burning. After filling comes to boil, continue to cook for 2 to 3 minutes, stirring constantly.
5. Remove from heat and whisk in the butter. If filling is being made ahead of time, refrigerate at this point and do the remaining steps on actual day of serving.
6. Stir in cognac.
7. Divide filling between two bowls. Add grated orange rind to one half, and grated lemon rind to other half.

Cake

METRIC/IMPERIAL

2kg/4½ lbs plain flour

2⅔ Tbsp baking powder

1.4kg/3 lbs margarine or butter

1.8kg/4 lbs sugar

2 dozen eggs

¼ litre/½ pint milk

4 tsp vanilla essence

AMERICAN

15 cups white flour

3⅓ Tbsp baking powder

6 cups margarine or butter

10 cups sugar

2 dozen eggs

1 cup milk

4 tsp vanilla

1. Preheat oven to 170°C/Gas Mark 4/350°F.
2. Rub baking tins with butter, then dust with flour. Use four tins, 48 x 38 x 4cm (19 x 15 x 1½in), or two bakery-sized sheet pans.
3. Sift flour and baking powder together. Set aside.
4. In a very large mixing bowl, cream together margarine and sugar until fluffy.
5. Add eggs one at a time and mix after each one.
6. If using an electric mixer, increase speed for 30 seconds, then turn down.
7. Alternate adding flour and milk.
8. Make sure everything is well mixed, scraping bottom and sides of mixture to centre of bowl with a spatula. As soon as ingredients are combined well, stop mixing.
9. Pour into baking tins and bake for 30 minutes, or until done.
10. Allow cake to cool completely, then remove from baking tins.

Puff Shells

1 litre/2 pints water

340g/12oz butter

4 tsp salt

450g/1 lb plain flour

16 eggs, at room temperature

a pastry bag with a 1.5cm (½in) open-ended nozzle

2 more eggs

4 cups water

3 cups butter

4 tsp salt

4 cups white flour

16 eggs, at room temperature

a pastry bag with a ½ inch open-ended nozzle

2 more eggs

1. Preheat oven to 220°C/Gas Mark 7/425°F.
2. Liberally rub four large baking tins with butter. (48 x 38 x 4cm or 19 x 15 x 1½in)
3. Sift flour and salt together. Set aside.
4. In a large saucepan, bring water to a boil with the butter. Continue boiling until butter has melted.
5. Remove from heat and add flour and salt all at once. Stir vigorously. Return to moderately high heat and cook, stirring constantly, just until mixture forms a ball that does not separate. Do not overcook.
6. Remove from heat. With a wooden spoon make a little well in the paste and break an egg into the centre of the well. Then beat egg into the paste until paste no longer looks slippery or shiny. Repeat this procedure with the rest of the 16 eggs. Towards the end it will take longer for each egg to be absorbed.
7. Spoon paste into pastry bag. Squeeze onto baking pan with a circular motion, so that each puff is round. Don't bother to flatten the points as these later catch the caramel as it is drizzled over the cake.

7

8. Make puffs in several sizes, the largest 2.5cm (1 inch), and the smallest half that size. The larger sizes are used for the bottom of the cake, graduating to the top, which uses very small puffs.

9. Beat 2 eggs with 1 Tbsp water. With a pastry brush apply beaten eggs just to the top of the puff. (If the egg goes too far down the side and touches the baking tin, it will keep the puff from rising.)

10. Bake puffs for about 20 minutes. When the puffs have doubled in size, are golden brown and firm to the touch, they are done.

11. Remove puffs from oven and cut a hole in the bottom of each one with the point of a knife. This hole will allow steam to escape and will be used to put cream into later.

12. Put the tray of puffs back into oven, with heat off and door ajar. Leave for at least 20 minutes. This will allow the puffs to dry out completely.

13. Do not fill puffs with cream until just before they are put on the cake, as they become soggy if filled too early.

9

11

Assembly

pattern pieces for cake: paper circles with the following diameters:

23cm (9in) two of each

20cm (8in) two of each

18cm (7in) two of each

15cm (6in) two of each

13cm (5in) two of each

10cm (4in) two of each

8cm (3in) two of each

5cm (2in) two of each

wooden cake base, with spindle 40cm (16in) high

2 bottles (70cl each) good quality cream sherry or Marsala or Madeira

2 litres/4 pints whipping cream

4 Tbsp each of 3 different fruit-flavoured liqueurs

680g/1½ lb sugared almonds

1 lb sugar

¼ litre/½ pint water

3 forks, held together with a rubber band

fresh flowers

1. Lay pattern pieces on cake and carefully cut cake with a small, sharp knife.
2. Prepare platform for cake by putting aluminium foil over base.
3. If any of the cake rounds are thicker than 2.5cm (1 inch), slice them in half.

AMERICAN

pattern pieces for cake: paper circles with the following diameters:

9in two of each

8in two of each

7in two of each

6in two of each

5in two of each

4in two of each

3in two of each

2in two of each

wooden cake base, with spindle 16in high

2 bottles (70cl each) good quality cream sherry or Marsala or Madeira

10 cups whipping cream

4 Tbsp each of 3 different fruit-flavoured liqueurs

1½ lb sugared almonds

2½ cups sugar

1¼ cups water

3 forks, held together with a rubber band

fresh flowers

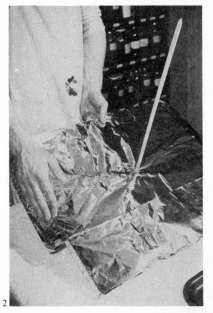
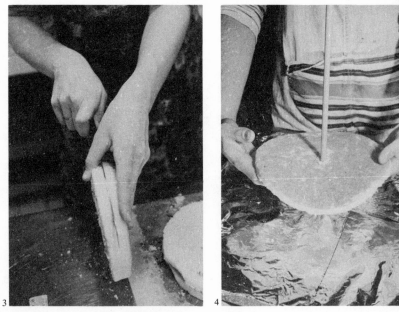

4. Carefully lower the largest cake round over the spindle, having first cut a hole in the centre with point of a knife.
5. Sprinkle the cake with sherry, controlling flow with a thumb over the opening of bottle. Be sure that the cake is well saturated but not mushy.
6. Spread the layer with filling.
7. Put the next layer on, being careful to centre one on top of the other.

8. Repeat the procedure with all layers, first sprinkling with sherry, then spreading with filling, alternating orange-flavoured filling with lemon-flavoured filling.
9. Whip the cream until stiff but not buttery.
10. Cover entire cake with whipped cream, just enough to cover the cakes and give a smooth well-shaped cone.
11. Divide remaining whipped cream into 3 batches. Flavour each batch with a different liqueur. Taste to see if the liqueur flavour can be noticed. Add a little more if necessary.

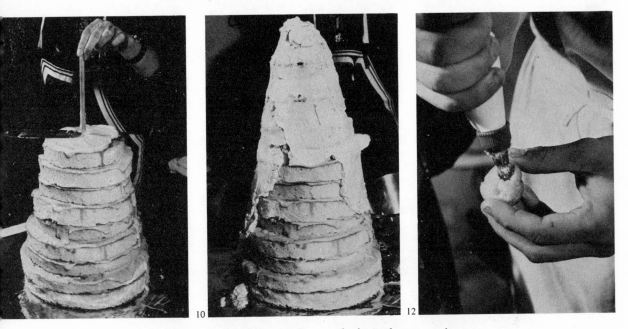

12. Fill each puff shell with flavoured whipped cream, using a pastry bag or a knife.
13. Beginning at the bottom with the largest ones, stick puffs onto the cake. Try not to have all of the puffs flavoured with one liqueur ending up in the same area of the cake; rather, have them roughly alternating. Finish with the very smallest puffs at the top.

14, Place sugared almonds here and there between the puffs. Tradition says that the almonds symbolise good luck.

15. For caramel syrup, place sugar and water in a saucepan and bring to a boil, stirring constantly. Let syrup cook until it turns light brown. Remove from heat.

16. As syrup is cooling, test occasionally to see if threads are forming yet.

19

17. When threads form, begin spinning a web around the cake, using three forks tied together. (If you wish to be extravagant, the best tool for this is a wire whisk with its top snipped off, leaving the ends sticking out.) At first it will appear that very little is happening.
18. As you continue to spin, however, the cake begins to take on a shimmer, and finally it becomes totally encased in shining threads.
19. The last step is to decorate the base with flowers.
20. Store the cake in a cool place until serving time.
21. To serve, scoop out 2 puffs and some cake for each person, using large silver serving spoons. As this is a very rich cake, each serving does not need to be very large.

About the Author

It was 1967 when I first discovered that vegetables do not grow in the frozen food section of the supermarket. While working as a United States Peace Corps volunteer in Venezuela, I was thrust into experiencing the mysterious world of the South American vegetable market in order to buy my food. The experience had a profound effect on me.

A few years after my return to the States, the natural food movement blossomed, and to my delight I discovered that people all around me were beginning to share my interest in 'real' food and unusual cookery. Years of recipe-trading sessions and cooking marathons led to teaching natural food cooking classes in my home state of California.

As part of a steadily deepening interest in spiritual matters, I visited the Findhorn Foundation in 1976. While stirring a pot of split pea soup in the Cluny Kitchen, I realised I was going to spend some time here.

I returned to Findhorn in 1978 as a member, and immediately began cooking in the community's kitchens. And I have found the experience to be a totally fulfilling one. Preparing meals for hundreds of people has been stimulating, challenging and rewarding. I have learned from the people I've cooked for, from the many guests who give of their talent and energy, from the food itself, and from the inspired and dedicated cooks of the Findhorn kitchens.

My thanks to all who have made this experience what it has been. And to people everywhere who are performing the sacred task of preparing food for their families: my blessings to you.

The Findhorn Foundation is an international spiritual community of about 250 members living and working in the north-east of Scotland. Founded in 1962 by Eileen and Peter Caddy and Dorothy Maclean, it initially attracted worldwide attention through its pioneering experiments in communicating with the nature kingdom. From there it has developed into an educational centre, receiving thousands of guests each year and broadening its work to include new approaches in the areas of government, education, spiritual growth, business, management, group dynamics and the arts.

Further information, including introductory material and tape and literature lists, is available on request. Write to:

Findhorn Publications
The Park, Findhorn
Forres IV36 OTZ
Scotland, U.K.

For those who would like to visit and take part in the work and life of the Foundation, we have an ongoing guest programme. Because of the increasing number of people wishing to visit the Findhorn Foundation you are advised to book as far in advance as possible. Accommodation cannot be guaranteed to those not booking. For booking and information regarding the guest programme, write to:

The Accommodation Secretary
Cluny Hill College
Forres IV36 ORD
Scotland, U.K.

Index